ALAN GAUNT

A QUIET AUTHORITY

GEORGE GAUNT - A LIFE

A QUIET AUTHORITY

GEORGE GAUNT - A LIFE

MEMOIRS

Cirencester

Published by Memoirs

MEMOIRS
PUBLISHING

25 Market Place, Cirencester, Gloucestershire, GL7 2NX
info@memoirsbooks.co.uk www.memoirspublishing.com

First published in England, April 2013

Book jacket design Ray Lipscombe

ISBN 978-1-909544-44-4

Printed in England

CONTENTS

DEDICATION

This book is dedicated to Bernard and Valerie

ACKNOWLEDGEMENTS

Many of those who have kindly helped me in the writing of this book are mentioned either in the main text or in the list of sources, but there are others who have been equally helpful and to whom I also owe a debt of gratitude: To all at Memoirs Publishing for providing polish and professionalism to my words; to Gordon Mckay who read the original drafts and provided wise and helpful comment; to Cllr Peter Jay of South Cerney Parish Council, who let me see the old Parish Council minutes; to Jody of Marstons PLC at Wolverhampton, who kindly gave me access to the Eliot Arms deeds packet; to Corporal Neil (Billy) Baxter of the Royal Anglian Regiment who provided an insight into Dad's job as Mess Steward; to the staff of the Templer Study Centre at the National Army Museum who introduced me to the mine of information that is the Household Brigade Magazine; to the staff at the Cirencester and Reading Libraries; and to Richard Fisher, whose knowledgeable website proved so helpful, and who generously allowed me to view his fascinating collection of machine gun artifacts. Finally, and by no means least, I must thank my wonderful wife Shirley who has helped, supported and advised me throughout the writing of this book.

INTRODUCTION

My interest in family history, and in particular the life of my father, George Gaunt, can be dated almost exactly. On the 8th February 1995, some 17 months after my mother had died, I received a letter from Don Grimshaw, a cousin on my father's side of the family. The letter is wonderfully written and is an item which I treasure. Don had been deputed by Dad's sister, Auntie Flo, who was then in her late eighties and the last surviving member of Dad's generation, to tell me that my father had been married before he met my mum and had had a family, about which I knew almost nothing.

I say 'almost' because after Mum passed away we found their marriage certificate, which revealed Dad to be 'the divorced husband of Evelyn Gaunt, formerly Dobson Spinster'. Having made this remarkable discovery, my Auntie Marjorie, Mum's sister, then told us that Dad had children from his previous marriage.

This fascinated and greatly intrigued Shirley, my wife, but it wasn't something to which I paid too much attention. I had other priorities in life - a growing family, a stressful job and my voluntary work as a school governor at my local school; and anyway I had not the vaguest idea about how to seek out or make contact with these relatives. Neither did I know if any such contact from me would be welcomed by them, so I did nothing.

However everything changed with the arrival of Don's letter, which gave a brief history of family events and confirmed not only that I had a brother but that he did indeed want to make contact. Amazed at this revelation, a meeting was accordingly arranged and, over the weekend of March 18th/19th 1995, I met my brother Bernard for the first time.

We spent the weekend at a Travel Inn near Tring in Hertfordshire with our families, getting to know each other. I was there with Shirley and our children, Stuart and Jenny; Bernard was with his wife, Jo, while Don was there with his wife Jean and Auntie Flo. It was an incredible time, with Bernard and I getting on wonderfully well despite the difference in age between us. Bernard was then 66, while I was 42, and I do think it very sad that we had not known each other much earlier. This age gap meant that although Bernard was my brother, he was effectively old enough to be my father. I do not think that difference was really important.

Don's letter also revealed that Bernard had a sister, Marion, but unfortunately I was never able to meet her. We did have an all-too-brief telephone conversation some while after I had met Bernard, but sadly she was not well and she eventually passed away in 1999.

A really surprising aspect of the talks and recollections that I had with Bernard is that in our father we remembered two different men. He remembered a fit, career-minded, hard-case disciplinarian Guards NCO, while I remembered a caring and loving family-minded father battling illness. I also found that Bernard had been trying to make contact with me at various times over the years but had been warned off each time by my mother. On one occasion in the early 1970s, he had even visited South Cerney and enquired at the local garage to find out where Mum and I lived. The man there gave him her address, pointed to my car disappearing over the River Churn bridge on the way to Cirencester and told him that he'd just missed meeting me face to face!

Calling at Mum's house in Station Road, Bernard was civilly received and given some old photographs of Dad, but she left him in no doubt that he had to be gone before I returned.

I have always known that Mum had been married before she met Dad, and that my half-sister Valerie had a different father to me. This matter was also largely common knowledge, but as to Dad's earlier life that was, in certain respects, a closed book. I shall never know why, but Mum and Dad had apparently decided that I should not be told about his first marriage and family, and despite Dad passing away in 1965, Mum kept her silence until the day she died twenty-eight years later.

Don's disclosure, and the long talks we had with Bernard, who had already started some family history research, prompted the start of my family history exploration. This began to reveal information about Dad's life, which in turn led to me writing this book. Here, then, is his story.

CHAPTER ONE

YORKSHIRE BEGINNINGS

See all, hear all, say nowt.
Eat all, sup all, pay nowt.
And if tha does owt for nowt,
Allus do it for thissen.
- traditional Yorkshire saying.

George Edward Gaunt was born on the 3rd December 1903 at
3 Longley Terrace in the village of Worsbrough Dale, south of
Barnsley in Yorkshire. He was the only child of Alfred Gaunt
and Sarah Ann, or Annie, Mewse. The couple had married at
Worsbrough Dale's Parish Church of St Thomas on 20th
December 1902; the church was quite modern, having been
built in 1859 as the village had expanded.

The marriage certificate shows Alfred's address simply as
'Worsbrough Dale' with no clue as to whereabouts in
Worsbrough Dale he might actually have lived or, indeed, with
whom he might have been living. However the certificate does
record William Edwards and Sarah Ann Edwards as witnesses
to the marriage, so it is possible that Alfred may have been

lodging with them, having moved from his family home some thirty miles away in Bramley, a village between Leeds and Bradford. Nevertheless, just what it was that prompted the move to Worsbrough Dale in particular remains a mystery.

Annie's address on the certificate is as vague as Alfred's, because it is simply shown as being 'Farsley Nr Bradford.' This village is also some thirty miles away from Worsbrough Dale. The box on the certificate showing her 'Rank or Profession' is struck through with a single line, which seems to indicate that she was not in work at the time of the wedding.

Although the marriage certificate described Alfred simply as a 'Labourer', he was probably working in a coal mine, because he was described on George's birth certificate, one year later, as a 'Colliery Labourer'. Worsbrough Dale was a well-developed mining village with a 1901 population of 10,335, but I have not been able to identify any particular mine where Alfred may have worked. The village was also the location of the Darley Main Colliery, which had suffered a disastrous explosion in 1874 when 75 men and boys were killed. Worsbrough Dale's other claim to fame is that it was the 1938 birthplace of Arthur Scargill, the controversial former President of the National Union of Mineworkers.

Alfred had not always been in the mines, having previously worked in a woollen mill. This had started when he was no more than 12, because the 5th April 1891 census had found him living at Lane End, Pudsey, a small market town next to Bramley, where he was described as a 'Bobbin setter at Worsted Mill.' (Worsted is a type of cloth using long wools). The more recent 1901 census, taken over the night of 31st

March that year, had shown him as living at 10 Victoria Row Bramley and working as a 'Woollen Mule Piecer'. A piecer's job was to repair, or piece together, the broken threads of wool on a spinning machine.

Alfred's father, Webster, had died from pneumonia on the 3rd April, shortly after the census, and it may have been this event which led to Alfred's move away from Bramley to Worsbrough Dale. However, there is no documentary evidence linking these events because I understand from the Probate Registry office in Leeds that Webster didn't leave a will.

Webster had broken with the long-standing Gaunt family tradition of working as clothiers and had spent most of his life as a tanner, making leather from the skins of animals. This is a smelly and unpleasant job which he had eventually left, before working briefly as a plasterer's labourer before his death at the age of 52. Webster's wife Martha survived him by some 2½ years before she died at the home of Alfred's younger brother, William in the mill town of Cleckheaton, about 10 miles from Pudsey, on 31st October, just over a month before George's birth. Martha Ann Farrar had been Webster's second wife; his first wife, Emily Briggs, had died of a fever shortly after their marriage.

At the time of the 1891 census, 11 year-old Annie Mewse had been staying with her grandparents in Derby Road, Felley, a village to the north of Nottingham. Her parents were living, at that particular time, at 5 Wheaters Yard, Pudsey, where her father, Robert, is described as being an 'Engine Fitter at Foundry.' However by the time of the 1901 census she was living with her parents at 4 Temperance Street, Farsley, which is presumably the address to which her marriage certificate refers. This was a couple of miles away from Bramley but a long way from Worsbrough Dale. Robert was still in the same job, or at least the same type of job, being then described as a 'Fitter at Iron Foundry' while being later described on Annie's marriage certificate as a 'Fitter'. Annie is described on the Census as a 'Twister at Woollen Mill.' The job of a twister was to produce a thread firm enough for weaving by drawing out and twisting the loose strands of wool.

Some time after George's birth, Alfred gave up mining, perhaps because of ill-health, and moved to live at 16 Balloon Row at the edge of Pudsey. Balloon Row was later renamed Bethel Terrace, presumably from the adjacent Bethel Chapel in Hough Side Road. However by 2007 all the houses there had been demolished and the site was being used for car parking.

It was while living here that George, when he was just over eighteen months old, was baptised in the Pudsey Trinity Wesleyan Methodist Chapel. This is an interesting choice of venue for George's baptism because I have found no significant history of Methodism in the Gaunt family, who appear to have generally been solidly Church of England, apart from some Non-Conformist baptisms in the early 19th Century. However Annie's parents were much more recently married in a Methodist chapel, so George's baptism would therefore seem to follow in the faith of his maternal, rather than his paternal, grandparents.

I think that to have her son baptised in the faith of her parents rather than that of her husband, as was much more usual at that time, points to a certain strength in Annie's character, a trait which I think George both inherited and admired.

4

Methodism had been founded in England following the preaching of John and Charles Wesley in the middle of the 18th Century. Their message was that salvation was possible for every believer, and that communion with God did not require the intervention of a priest. The Methodist chapel in which George was baptised had been opened comparatively recently, on the 1st May 1899, and at a cost of £7,700 was Pudsey's most expensive place of non-conformist worship. It had been built to replace a much older chapel on the site which had been considered insufficiently grand for use as a principle place of worship and accordingly demolished to make way for this new building. The new chapel continued in use until it was closed in 1982, but the building survives; it is in use now as an arts centre and shopping mall.

Once in Bramley, Alfred returned to mill work and got a job as a mule spinner in a woollen mill. The spinning mule on which he worked was a water-powered machine invented by Samuel Crompton in 1778 and which combined a water frame and a spinning jenny. It was called a 'mule' because it was a hybrid machine containing features of these two different systems. Alfred's job was to operate the machinery. A report in the late 19th Century had argued that 'to be effectively managed the mule must be minded by men and boys, who are stronger, more suitably clad, and have more staying power than women.'

Life in the woollen mill was hard, with long working hours. At one mill, the weekday hours were 7 am - 8.30 am, followed by a break for breakfast from 8.30 am to 9 am, and the next shift lasting from 9 am - 12.30 pm. Dinner was from 12.30 - 1.30, with afternoon hours lasting from 1.30 - 5.15. On Saturdays work lasted from 7 – 12 noon, with breakfast from 8.30 – 9.

There were numerous mills in the area, and many of Alfred's relatives had worked in the clothing industry. The Allan Brigg Mill in Lane End, Pudsey, was very close to Balloon Row, and it is possible that Alfred worked there. Certainly the Gaunt family's connections with the area around Lane End were long established, and the family had been clothiers in the area since the 18th Century or even earlier. By the time of the 1841 Census, for example, there were five families by the name of Gaunt living in Lane End alone, including Alfred's 55 year-old great grandfather, John Gaunt, who is described as a clothier. He is later described on the 1861 Census as a 'Handloom Woollen Weaver,' whilst his death certificate on 16th December 1866, when he was described as being 82, confirmed his cause of death as 'Old Age Certified'.

The trade of clothier had been continued by Alfred's grandfather, Samuel Gaunt, who is listed variously over the years as a 'Wool Weaver' or a 'Cloth Weaver'. Although a widower - his wife Frances had died in 1888 - Samuel worked hard at his job and had made enough money to provide for himself in retirement, being described on the 1901 Census as residing in a two-room dwelling and 'living on own means.' His address at that time was in an area of Pudsey known as Crimbles, which was close to Lane End, and he may well have been living there when Alfred and his family arrived from Worsbrough Dale. Samuel was eventually admitted to the Union Workhouse and Infirmary about eight miles away at Clayton, where he is recorded as having died of 'senile decay' at the age of 84 on the 24th April 1907.

On the 29th August 1905, just over two months after

George's baptism, his father, then aged only 26, sadly died from pulmonary tuberculosis. Alfred's death certificate shows that Balloon Row, although situated at the edge of Pudsey township, actually fell within the area covered by the Bramley Registration District. At some point thereafter, probably during the latter part of 1905 or early 1906, George's mother met and went to live with Alfred Grimshaw, who was described on the previous census in 1901 as being a 'Riveter (Boiler)'. Alfred's wife had gone off and left him with two children to bring up: Sarah Ann, born in November 1890 and Leonard, born in January 1893. The 1901 Census had also shown him and the children living with his parents, Amos and Christiana, at 1 Back Wood Street, Rodley. This is the next village to Bramley and the street was close to the Leeds/Liverpool canal. However Amos died in 1903 and Christiana died in 1905, so Alfred had found himself looking after the children on his own.

It is not too difficult to imagine the scenario where a widow with a young child would seek employment as housekeeper to a man trying to look after two children in the absence of his wife. This was quite probably the initial situation with Annie and Alfred, but it quickly grew into something more personal despite the age difference - by 1906 Alfred was 39 and Annie was 27. Although not an everyday occurrence, these circumstances were apparently not unique. Alison Maloney's book *Life Below Stairs* records that 'Widowed or single men of means often had a housekeeper who would provide the most basic functions of a housewife, keeping the home clean, cooking meals, looking after children and, in some cases, even sharing the bed.' Whilst I know of no evidence to suggest that

Alfred Grimshaw could be described as a man of means, the circumstances detailed in Ms. Maloney's book certainly seem to have applied in this case.

Alfred and Annie firstly lived at 8 Wood Street, Rodley, which was on the other side of Back Wood Street where Alfred had lived with his parents. These streets ran between Rodley Town Street and the canal, and it was here at number 8, on the 14th March 1907, that Alfred and Annie's first child, Florrie (otherwise known as Flo) was born. Alfred is described on Flo's birth certificate as now being a 'Forge Labourer'. The forge is the place where metal is heated until it is sufficiently soft for it to be hammered into a different shape which it then retains, so working on a forge can be hot, heavy and tiring. It is hardly surprising therefore that Alfred should seek help with looking after the home. Alfred wasn't divorced from his wife so he couldn't marry Annie, who is described on the birth certificate as 'Sarah Ann Gaunt formerly Mewse a Housekeeper (Domestic Servant).'

Flo was baptised on the 8th September 1907 and Leonard Grimshaw, now 14 years old, was baptised at the same time. This event took place in the nearby Parish Church of St Wilfred in Calverley, because Rodley formed part of the original Calverley Parish. The Baptism Register entry records Annie Grimshaw as the mother to both Flo and Leonard. The family then moved to 5 Cowley Road, Rodley, a stone built back-to-back terraced house on a short street sloping up from Rodley Town Street about a quarter of a mile away from Wood Street.

Alfred and Annie's second child, Lyndhurst (also known as Lyn), was born here on 9th August 1909. The birth certificate again described Annie as 'Housekeeper (Domestic Servant)' while Alfred continues to be described as a 'Forge Labourer'.

There is no personal record of what life was like for Alfred Grimshaw and his family at this time, but perhaps a partial glimpse may be gained from a survey of Leeds schoolchildren in the early years of the century. This showed that a typical child's breakfast consisted of white bread and treacle with tap water or weak tea. The main meal of the day would often comprise black pudding, liver and onions, a stew called 'penny duck' consisting of offal meat or fish, or tinned meat with pickles and chips. Although not a meal in itself, a particular 'Yorkshire delicacy' which I remember Dad enthusing about, and to which both Bernard and I are very partial, is fruitcake eaten with a slice of cheese. Delicious!

Houses were generally sparsely furnished, with clip-rugs scattered over the floors. These were made of strips of old cloth and clothes pushed through a canvas base. If the house had a cellar, this would serve both as a food store and a coal store. It could also house the copper where the water was boiled on washday - usually a Monday. The focus of family life, however, was the fire, often part of a large black-leaded range which provided cooking facilities as well as hot water.

The 1911 Census, taken for the night of Sunday 2nd April, shows Alfred and Annie together with their children next living at Warley View, Rodley Road, Bramley. Warley View takes its name from a General Warley, who commanded Civil War troops camped in the area and whose white-coated uniforms gave the locality its name of Whitecote. The house where Alfred and Annie lived was number 30 Warley View, which forms part of a short terrace of houses close to the junction of Rodley Road and the Leeds-Bradford Road and is about midway between Bramley and Rodley. It was constructed of cement rendered walls under a slate roof and had four rooms. It was an all-through terraced house with the additional advantage of a good-sized front garden. This represented a considerable improvement both in terms of living conditions and social status compared to the back-to-back houses where the family had lived previously.

Leonard Grimshaw was no longer there in 1911, but the presence of Alfred's daughter, Sarah Ann Grimshaw, from his broken marriage indicates that she had probably always lived with them. She is now 20 years old and employed as a worsted spinner. Annie Gaunt's relationship with Alfred is described on the census form as 'Servant' while her personal occupation is described as 'Housekeeper'. Seven-year-old George is described as Alfred's brother. Living at Warley View must have been something of an omen for George because, as a Coldstream Guardsman in the 1930s, he would be stationed at Warley Barracks, many miles away in Essex.

The Census in 1911 described George as a 'Scholar', although it has been difficult to fully trace his education and none of the admission registers for schools in the area have survived. However his later Army documents do show that he attended the Council School in Bramley. The 1906 Ordnance Survey map shows this school to have stood close to the junction of Broad Lane with Whitecote Hill and Upper Town Street, so it was near to the addresses where George lived, both in Warley View and later in Broad Lane itself. It was a new school which was opened in September 1900 at a cost of £9,000, having been built to accommodate 650 pupils. According to the Bramley History Society, the school probably closed in the 1980s and was later converted into flats. However, despite this change, former pupil Brian Dean says that it 'still maintains its stunning looks'.

George could have started at this school in 1909 when he was five, but it is more likely that he started at Rodley Infants' School, which was very close to the Cowley Road address where the family was living that year. He could then have either moved up the hill to the Broad Lane school when the family moved to Warley View in about 1910 or he could have transferred to Broad Lane from the Rodley school when he reached the age of ten.

Alfred is described on the census form as an 'Iron Miller in Crane Foundry' so he may have worked at either the nearby Union Foundry or the Old Foundry, both in Rodley Town Street and bordering the Leeds/Liverpool Canal. The Union Foundry was owned by Joseph Booth & Bros, established in 1847, while The Old Foundry was owned by Thomas Smith and Sons, founded in 1820. *Whitakers Red Book of Commerce or Who's Who in Business* for 1914 described both firms as being crane manufacturers, although only Joseph Booth has the additional description of 'Engineers.' The two companies were later to merge.

The Union Foundry of Joseph Booth & Bros is closest to Alfred's previous addresses and is where he could have been working as a Forge Labourer, so I think it more likely that he worked here rather than at Thomas Smith's. Additionally it has been recorded that the houses in Back Wood Street (and presumably those in Wood Street itself) were demolished, probably during the mid-20th Century, to provide a car park for Booth's Crane Works. Therefore the houses may have already been owned by Booth's and could well have been used to house their workers. Accordingly, and as Alfred lived there, I think it is reasonable to assume that he was employed by Booths. My wife Shirley and I visited the site in 2007 but the Foundry and all around had apparently been demolished in 1999, and the area was undergoing a lot of redevelopment.

On the 11th April 1914, when Sarah Ann Grimshaw married Alfred Broughton at the Parish Church of St Johns in the adjoining Parish of Wortley-de-Leeds, the family was living about a mile away from Warley View at 277 Broad Lane Bramley. Sarah is simply described on the marriage certificate (somewhat undiplomatically I think) as a 'Twister' which is another name for the 'Worsted Spinner' description of her employment shown on the 1911 Census form. She could well have been employed at St Catherine's Worsted Mill, which is close by, just off Broad Lane. Alfred is presumably still working at Joseph Booth's, because he is described on the certificate as an 'Iron Miller'.

It could have been while at this address that as an 11 year-old, George attended Bramley's Moriah Primitive Methodist Sunday School. I can find no record of Methodism in the recent background of Alfred Grimshaw, so George's attendance at this Sunday school would seem to be due to Annie keeping him in the faith to which he was baptised. It was at the Sunday school, in January 1915, that he was awarded a copy of Jules Verne's book *Twenty Thousand Leagues Under The Sea* in recognition of his 'punctual attendance.' I still have this book, which was first published in 1869 and tells the tale of Captain Nemo and his submarine the *Nautilus*. The book was made into a film in 1954 starring Kirk Douglas, with James Mason playing the role of Captain Nemo.

The Methodist Chapel Sunday School which George attended was a tall, imposing building situated just off Bramley Town Street. Along with much of the original village of Bramley, it has since been demolished and replaced by sprawling 20th Century housing. It was during this period, or perhaps a little later, that George also took a part-time job in a barber's shop, but he often had to also look after his half-brother Lyn, sitting, and sometimes sleeping, in the corner of the shop. Lyn often said in later years that this always led to him associating visits to the barber's with going to sleep!

The family was to move at least once more. By the time George was 14 they had moved the short distance to 270 Broad Lane Bramley. It was here on 22nd May 1918 that his mother died at the age of 38 from 'Pulmonary Tuberculosis, General Exhaustion' and 'Cardiac Failure'. Living conditions at that time will have been particularly hard, thanks to strict wartime rationing which had been introduced earlier in the year. However shortages of general household items, as well as essential foodstuffs such as bread and meat, had been keenly felt as early as 1916, and this may well have been a contributing factor to Annie's weakened state and ill health. I also believe that her particular family circumstances could easily have placed her under an additional strain. Certainly, for one reason or another, she and Alfred appear to have been almost constantly on the move, living in no fewer than five different houses over a period of about eleven years, which cannot have been easy for her.

The death certificate for Annie shows her name as 'Sarah Gaunt otherwise Grimshaw,' which indicates that she was effectively regarded locally as 'Mrs. Grimshaw' despite the lack of a marriage certificate. Her 'Rank or Profession' however is stated as 'Housekeeper Widow of Alfred Gaunt a Woollen Millhand', and it is likely that she was buried, probably along with her husband Alfred, in the graveyard at St Peter's Church Bramley. This church, which originally dated from about 1861, was almost completely rebuilt in 1978-1979, with only the belfry and spire remaining from the original. It seems that the graveyard must have been largely cleared at about that time, because there were very few graves remaining when we visited in 2007. Instead of finding a large Victorian graveyard where we might have stood a chance of finding the grave, we were disappointingly confronted with a public park simply containing some random clusters of gravestones.

Annie's death left Alfred Grimshaw, at the age of 51, once again having to look after children on his own. Flo was now 11 but Lyn was only eight, and both were still of school age, probably attending the Broad Lane School along with George. However, as George was older and able to do more to help, he had to leave school and get a job in a factory to bolster the family income and help to provide for Lyn and Flo.

I remember him telling me about this period in his life and saying that he had been only 14 when he had to leave school. This means he would have left school early, because the leaving age at Broad Lane was normally 15 unless the pupil had taken the Eleven-Plus exam to go on to a high school in Leeds.

I also remember him telling me that when at work he was given some horrible jobs to do including, on one occasion, cleaning up the mess after a worker's head had been crushed in a horrific accident. It is entirely possible that George went to work at the same place as Alfred, which was probably Joseph Booth's 'Union Foundry'. George's 1925 Annual Report form for the Coldstream Guards described his 'trade or calling before enlistment' as 'Turner', which is a key role in manufacturing and engineering companies. A turner works with a lathe which shapes the metal being worked upon and, amongst other things, makes items for conveyor, hydraulic and pneumatic devices such as those produced by Joseph Booth & Brothers. Qualification for the job of turner often followed an apprenticeship which could last for seven years, and this could explain why George eventually left in 1925, having presumably completed, or neared the end, of his apprenticeship, but also having decided that life in a factory was not for him.

The family must have started to break up some time after Annie died, because Flo was sent away to live with relatives in Nottingham, although I have no information on the exact date of this event. Her maternal grandparents, Robert Mewse and Jane Elizabeth Dickerson, had been married there in the Tennyson Street Methodist Chapel in September 1879, and Flo's mother had been born in Annesley, a village just outside Nottingham, shortly afterwards in the following October.

Robert Mewse came from the village of Barnack in Northamptonshire, which is close to the border with Lincolnshire and the town of Stamford, where his family originated. Although his work took him around the country, he was still in the Nottingham area for the birth of two sons, George in 1880 and Frank in 1883, but was in Leicester when his third son Robert was born in 1887. He had then moved to the Pudsey area, where daughters Frances and Ethel were born in 1890 and 1893 respectively, before moving on to the adjacent village of Farsley, where he was living in 1901. At some point thereafter he had returned to Nottingham, living in Fisher Street and working as a lace machine fitter until his death in 1910 from TB at the age of 52.

His widow, Jane Elizabeth, was still in Nottingham, where she lived in Bateman Street and then Grimston Street before being admitted to the Infirmary in Hucknall Road where she died in 1929. There were also various other relatives in the city, and it was almost certainly this branch of the family to whom Flo was sent to be brought up.

Unfortunately I know nothing about two of the aunts who looked after Flo, except that they were apparently both very strict. However, one aunt who helped to raise Flo, and with whom Flo lived when she was older, was Ivy Hartshorn, who at one point lived in Carlton, a suburb of Nottingham. The Hartshorn and Mewse families had joined in 1889 when Flo's Great Aunt, Elizabeth Ann Mewse, had married Samuel Hartshorn in the Nottingham suburb of Basford. I don't know why Flo should have been sent away; it may have been considered better for her to be brought up with female influence rather than in the all-male household in which she had lately lived.

CHAPTER TWO

THE COLDSTREAM GUARDS

'Nulli Secundus' ('Second to None') -
the motto of the Coldstream Guards

The next to leave home was George. On the 14th April 1925 at the age of 21, he enlisted in the Coldstream Guards at the Army Recruiting Office in Clarendon Road, Leeds. The first act of the enlistment process required George to attend before a magistrate to swear an oath of loyalty to King George V and to his successors and to observe and obey the orders of the King's Generals and Officers.

George is described at the time as being 5' 11" tall and weighing 139 lbs; his eyes are grey, his hair is fair, his complexion is fresh and he has no distinctive marks. His religion is listed as 'Primitive Methodist'. The attestation (enrolment) forms list George's next of kin as his 'Stepfather Alfred Grimshaw.' This, I think, points to Alfred being perhaps much more of a father-like figure to George, and not merely his mother's employer, as appeared to be indicated by some of the documents quoted earlier. There is no evidence to show why George chose to join the Coldstream Guards in particular, but Leeds was traditionally amongst the Coldstream Guards' best recruiting areas, so this may well have influenced his decision.

The Coldstream Guards were first known as Colonel Monck's Regiment of Foot, being raised in 1650 as part of Oliver Cromwell's New Model Army. When Charles II became King in 1660 the New Model Army was disbanded, apart from Monck's Regiment, which had marched to London from its home town of Coldstream to restore order in the capital before the king's return. It was then decided to incorporate the Regiment into the King's own Guards, and this was undertaken on the 14th February 1661. The regiment was paraded on Tower Hill next to the Tower of London and ordered to lay down their weapons as soldiers of the New Model Army and to then pick them up as the Lord General's Regiment of Foot Guards. This dates the start of the Regiment's history as personal guards to the Sovereign. They were then listed in the Sovereign's service as the Second Regiment of Foot Guards, but the men of the regiment would not accept this title because they belonged to an older unit than the First Regiment. Accordingly they initially adopted the motto 'Nulli Secundus' and, in 1670, the title 'Coldstream Guards'.

The Regiment had a minimum height standard for recruits of 5' 9", which was specified in its standing orders, although the figure could be varied at the discretion of the Regimental Lieutenant Colonel. George was tall enough to comfortably pass this test, so he signed on for the normal three years as a soldier with the Colours and three years in the Reserves. He was sent from Leeds straight to the Guards Depot at Caterham in Surrey, and his journey to this famous depot was probably by train to London, then on the local train to Caterham followed by a walk up the steep hill to the barracks. These had been built in 1877 at a cost of £46,273, but they ceased to be used as a training depot in 1960 and were replaced by new facilities elsewhere in the County, at Pirbright.

Shirley and I had planned to visit the barracks site at Caterham to see what it looked like, but we decided against it when we discovered that the last of the Guards had moved out in 1995 and that it had been subsequently and extensively re-developed for housing.

Following his arrival at Caterham, George was allocated the Army number 2652062 and spent the first six months of his Army career undergoing the rigorous disciplinary training of the Guards as a member of Corporal G S Butler's squad. The introduction to his training will have reinforced his conviction that he had chosen to join an élite unit; the *Notes for Lecturers to Recruits of the Brigade of Guards* stated that 'No body of troops in the world, now or in the past, has ever had finer traditions, a more glorious record, or a higher standard than the Brigade of Guards. The Brigade has always set an example of efficiency, discipline, smartness and soldierly qualities both in war and peace which soldiers of our own or any other army should be proud to follow.'

Life at the barracks was tough; barrack rooms were crowded and spartan, containing 20 iron beds, each with three coir 'biscuits' for a mattress. The day started at 6 am, the 'Notes for Lecturers' instructing that 'Men will rise at reveille, shave, wash and make up their beds. The windows will be opened at reveille in the summer and at 7.45 am in the winter. Beds will be made up half an hour after reveille'. Food was filling although rather plain, and discipline was rigid. There was an evening 'shining parade' when recruits cleaned and polished their equipment and were grilled on all aspects of regimental history including battle honours, names of commanding officers over the years and recognition of bugle calls. This parade was scheduled to end at 7 pm but could often last much longer. It was then followed, before 'lights-out' at 10 pm, by a rigorous hand and foot inspection.

During George's time at Caterham he will have had to take part in the daily 6.30 am 'Breakfast Parade' held before the 7 am breakfast. This was no ordinary parade but, astonishingly, a 'punishment' which had been introduced personally by Queen Victoria. She had once been horrified to see a Guardsman whose turnout was not up to the standard that she expected of her Guards. Accordingly she ordered that all five regiments of the Guards should hold an early morning punishment parade for one hundred years which, over time, became known as the 'Breakfast Parade'. Each day on the barrack-square parade ground a different piece of uniform or equipment had to be shown to the Inspecting Officer to demonstrate that it met the Brigade's high standards. The parade was eventually withdrawn during the 1950s, presumably at the expiry of the one hundred years specified by the Queen.

In addition to the constant drill and military training, George was able to resume his education and, on the 15th July, he gained his Third Class Army Certificate of Education. This must have been a general test, because the Certificate does not list any specific subjects covered by the exam. Apart from training and educational requirements, the living arrangements of soldiers were subject to the imposition of equally high standards and, according to a list of punishments in the 1920s, a soldier could be punished just for having a 'dirty bed-space'. The Notes for Lecturers went on to state that soldiers 'will take pride in the cleanliness of their barrack-rooms, and, besides keeping their own things perfectly clean and in order, they will be most careful not to dirty the room by upsetting blacking etc., while they are 'shining' or grease while they are having their dinners. All their clothing will be neatly folded on their shelves, all their kit clean, their beds properly made up, their boxes clean and tidy, and everything should be perfectly ready in case of having to turn out suddenly.'

There was also a constant changing of uniform - khaki and buff equipment for drill, vest and shorts for physical training, khaki undress for education, canvas overalls and web equipment for musketry and back to khaki for the second drill period. Uniforms were required to be immaculate; the 'Notes for Lecturers' ruled that 'Soldiers should take the greatest pride in their smartness in every way. It must be their constant thought to turn out not only themselves but also every article of clothing, arms and accoutrements spotlessly clean and smart'.

Achieving this objective was not helped, for example, by the lack of irons. Soldiers could only attain the 'knife-edge' creases demanded for their uniform by carefully folding it, then placing it under the mattress overnight while sleeping on it.

Apart from keeping their accommodation immaculate and their clothing spotlessly clean, the soldiers were also lectured on the benefits of health and personal cleanliness; the 'Lecturer's Notes' stated 'It is the absolute duty of every soldier to do all in his power to keep himself healthy, for a man who is not strong and healthy can neither march nor fight, and a soldier is of no use unless he can do both.' In a brief foretaste of much later action to restrict smoking, the 'Notes' also warned against 'excessive cigarette smoking, which may ruin a man's constitution.' They then went on to state: 'Soldiers will pay the most scrupulous attention to cleanliness. No man is good for much who has not proper self-respect, and no man can be self-respecting if he is dirty. Washing is also necessary to health; nothing is more healthy than cold water and plenty of it.' In a rather less hardy age, and much preferring the benefits of hot water, that last statement does indeed make me shiver.

The 'Notes for Lecturers' also explained the reasoning behind the imposition of very strict discipline at the depot, stating: 'Lastly, it must never be forgotten that the strict discipline under which every man in the army is placed is not insisted on without a good reason. Without discipline it would be impossible to have control over any body of men in action, and the strict discipline in regard to small matters in barracks and on parade is the means of teaching the absolute and immediate obedience which is the basis of discipline that gives a commander control over his men in action and that wins battles.'

The depot's strict régime was also acknowledged in the wider community. There is a story of one recruit arriving at Caterham and receiving directions to the depot from a plumber who told him 'When you get to the top of the hill you will see two gates. The one on the left is for the lunatic asylum, the other is the entrance to the barracks. Young man, take my advice and take the gate on the left!'

Notwithstanding this particular piece of advice, many Guardsmen who passed through the Depot would look back on their time at Caterham, if not fondly, then at least with gratitude, and I suspect that George would have been amongst them. They have spoken of the good food, the well-arranged training, the regimental initiatives and the games. One particular attraction of the Depot, recalled by a recruit, was that 'You can go to Croydon and see the great aerodrome and aeroplanes landing'. However the general attitude of those who went through the Depot is perhaps best summed up in a quote from the book *The Guards and Caterham*, which states: 'I have never met a Guardsman who regretted his days at the old Guards Depot, Caterham.'

On the 13th October 1925 George completed his training period at Caterham and was posted to the 1st Battalion of the Coldstream Guards, stationed at Wellington Barracks in London. George had impressed his instructors while at Caterham, and he continued to impress his new superiors in London; his first report on 24th November described his 'Military Conduct' as 'very good' and went on to state that 'This recruit came from the Depot with a very good record' and 'he has done well since he has been in No 1 Company.' Apart from their ceremonial duties, the Guards served as infantry; the battalion's structure was therefore similar to that of a typical infantry regiment. Accordingly George would have been allocated to a rifle section of around ten men commanded by a Corporal or Lance Sergeant (a rank peculiar to the Guards). Three sections would customarily have formed a platoon commanded by a junior officer, while three or more platoons would form the company of which he was a member, and which was under the command of a captain or major. The 1st Battalion is therefore likely to have consisted of three such rifle companies, together with a headquarters company and a machine gun company which contained the particular weapons considered too important to attach to the rifle companies.

Wellington Barracks is located in Birdcage Walk, which is only a short distance from Buckingham Palace. This fact made the barracks a popular base for the soldiers because it reduced the length of the march from there when undertaking public duty at the Palace. The barracks were originally built in 1833 in a neoclassical style and named Westminster Guards Barracks, being later renamed and altered to provide accommodation for two battalions. They continue to be occupied by units of the Foot Guards and to house their regimental headquarters. It was while he was stationed here that George experienced his first taste of the Guards' extensive ceremonial duties by taking part in the Changing of the Guard Ceremony, or 'Guard Mounting' as it is also known.

As a fully-fledged member of the King's personal guard, George wore the renowned 'Guard Order' uniform when undertaking these assignments. The uniform consisted of a scarlet tunic, which at that time had white leather cross belts holding a greatcoat on the back, folded as an oblong, with a rolled cape underneath, a bayonet to the side and ammunition pouches to the front. It had blue trousers with a red stripe down the side over spotlessly shiny boots, and the entire ensemble was crowned by a tall bearskin cap. The design of the uniform identified him as a member of the Coldstream Guards, with the buttons on the front of the tunic being grouped in pairs, a Garter Star decorating the tunic collar and a scarlet plume showing on the right side of the bearskin.

If George felt any hint of nerves in his smart uniform and taking part in his first public ceremonial, he could at least take consolation from the fact that the rest of those in the battalion were either equally new to the ceremony or hadn't been involved in it for some time; this was because the battalion itself had only just arrived at the barracks after an absence of three years. *Household Brigade Magazine* reported that 'mounting guard certainly came a bit strange, but we have become quickly acclimatised, and already feel seasoned soldiers in this respect'.

The original Guard Mounting ceremony dates from the late 17th Century, but the procedure in which George was a participant dated from about 1837, when Queen Victoria began to use Buckingham Palace as London's principle royal residence. It involves a parade with the Regimental Band from Wellington Barracks to both Buckingham Palace and the nearby St James' Palace, where the various guards are changed over. The most significant difference between George's time and the current ceremony is that the soldiers guarding Buckingham Palace were then positioned outside the Palace railings, so George would have had the difficult job of patrolling his 'beat' through the milling crowds of tourists.

However, following an incident in 1959 when a tourist was kicked by a guardsman, the Guards were moved inside the railings. These tourists would also congregate along the railings outside Wellington Barracks, and it was commented that despite concentrated instruction on weapon training or drill, the young guardsman could apparently still find 'his thoughts and vision wandering' to the watching ladies in the crowd.

Other public duties fell to the battalion, and a detachment of 125 all ranks were sent to take part in the 11th November Armistice Day ceremony at the Cenotaph. This had been introduced in 1919 to commemorate the ending of the First World War. Later that month the battalion was next called upon to provide men for the Guard of Honour at the funeral service in Westminster Abbey of Queen Alexandra. She was the widow of King Edward VII and was buried alongside her husband in St Georges Chapel, Windsor.

Now that George was away in London with the Coldstream Guards, Flo was living in Nottingham and Lyn still in Leeds, the family seemed to have completely broken up. But George kept them together. He used to divide his leave periods between Nottingham and Leeds, bringing presents, news and instructions for Flo and Lyn to write to each other. He became younger brother Lyn's role model, and I have been told that Lyn would often say in later life that George was more of a father to him than his real one.

George's education continued at his new station and he passed his Second Class Army Certificate of Education on the 26th March 1926. This time the certificate lists the subjects covered by the exam as English, Mathematics and Map

Reading. Shortly thereafter the battalion were busy rehearsing for the King's Birthday Parade, which is more commonly known as 'Trooping the Colour', but both the rehearsals and the ceremony were cancelled by the nine-day General Strike, which was called during the early part of May.

When not on duty guarding Government offices in the Whitehall area during this time, troops of the battalion were confined to Wellington Barracks, which they were required to share with men and armoured cars of the Royal Tank Corps brought in from Lydd in Kent. The only break in the monotony of the soldier's confinement was provided by games held in Green Park, which were described as 'a very welcome and much needed boon.'

The Battalion moved to Pirbright in Surrey for two months before going to London's Chelsea Barracks in August 1926. These barracks had been built in the 1860s and were designed to house two battalions of troops. They were much less in the public eye than Wellington Barracks and the large barrack square was also enclosed by buildings, providing a more private environment for the Guards to practise their drill. These original brick-built Victorian buildings were replaced in the middle of the 20th Century by concrete tower blocks, which were demolished after the Army moved out. When I saw the site in March 2012 it was surrounded by high fences pending extensive redevelopment.

During his time at Chelsea, on the 27th September 1926, George was appointed to the rank of Lance Corporal. This rank is usually signified by the wearing of a single white chevron on the right sleeve, but not in the Brigade of Guards.

Queen Victoria had decreed that single chevrons should not be worn by her Foot Guards so, uniquely to the Guards, a Lance Corporal's rank is denoted by two chevrons. George's appointment as Lance Corporal was then followed on 30th September by his being granted permission to extend his service to complete seven years with the Colours and five years in the Reserves.

The 1920s were marked by the unveiling of a myriad war memorials up and down the country in commemoration of those in the armed forces who had lost their lives during the First World War. Amongst these many unveiling ceremonies was that carried out by His Royal Highness Prince Arthur Duke of Connaught on the 16th October 1926 at the Guards Memorial in Horse Guards Parade London, commemorating the many thousands of guardsmen who died in the war. Prince Arthur, born in 1850, had been the favourite son of Queen Victoria and Godson to the Duke of Wellington. He had commanded the Guards Brigade at the battle of Tel el Kebir during the 1882 invasion of Egypt, and was currently the Brigade's senior Colonel, so he had been asked by his nephew, King George V, to undertake the unveiling ceremony.

After the ceremony, a huge march-past took place involving some sixteen thousand serving and ex-service guardsmen - a mixture of scarlet, khaki and civilian dress. There was scarlet from the ten battalions of the Guards, including the 1st Battalion Coldstream Guards with which George was serving, khaki from the Brigade of Guards detachments representing the wartime Guards Division and civilian dress from the old comrades marching behind each battalion. The march-past of the Memorial is reported to have taken forty minutes to complete and must have been an extraordinary sight. By remarkable coincidence, the number of men taking part in the march-past approximated to the total number of men in the Division who had been killed during the War and whose memory they were commemorating.

By the time of his Annual Report on the 31st October 1926, George was a member of the Battalion's Machine Gun Platoon, his job being described as a Machine Gunner. The report stated that he tried hard and was intelligent, and that, although he had only been appointed to the rank of Lance Corporal as recently as 26th September, George promised to be 'a very good NCO'.

The gun he would have been operating was a .303 Vickers machine gun weighing 40 lbs and mounted on a tripod. It was fed by a fabric ammunition belt holding 250 rounds and was capable of firing some 500 rounds per minute. Adopted for use by the British Army in 1912, the gun had proved to be extremely effective during the First World War and was to remain in service until 1968.

It was certainly formidable, being officially listed as having a range of some 4,500 yards. This meant that it could be used not only defensively, by helping to protect key positions against attacking infantry, but perhaps more importantly as an offensive weapon against enemy positions which could be as far away as an incredible 2½ miles. George would therefore have been trained to use the gun as a sort of 'light artillery', harassing enemy movement by sending plunging barrage fire against their distant road systems, trenches and troop assembly areas. This particular use of the gun contrasts quite sharply with its general portrayal in films and television, where it is almost always shown as a simple short-range defensive weapon.

The Guards Machine Gun Regiment, formed during World War One, had been disbanded in 1922 and the guns returned to the individual Guards battalions, where they were grouped into separate Machine Gun Companies. The Army's *Small Arms Training Manual* of 1931, which dates from the time when George was a Machine Gunner, describes such a company in peacetime as comprising a headquarters and three platoons, with each platoon consisting of a platoon headquarters and two sections. The platoon was commanded by a junior officer known as a subaltern, with a sergeant (the Platoon Sergeant) as second-in-command.

Apart from the platoon commander and his sergeant, the platoon headquarters consisted of an observer, an orderly and two scouts, all of whom were trained machine-gunners. Each of the sections in the platoon consisted of about 12 men commanded either by a sergeant or a lance sergeant, together with a second-in-command and assisted in their headquarters group by a range taker and an orderly, the rest of the section being made up of two sub-sections of about four men, each manning a single machine gun. Number 1 in the sub-section was the leader. He fired the gun while Number 2 controlled the entry of the ammunition belts into the gun's feed-block, Number 3 maintained a supply of ammunition to Number 2 and Number 4 was a carrier. All the members of the team were fully trained in handling the gun.

George's appointment to this key specialist post was almost

certainly influenced by his engineering background and his formal training as a turner. The Vickers Machine Gun was a complex piece of weaponry which comprised over 130 parts machined from high-grade steel, and George had to know all of these parts and how they worked, how they were maintained and how they fitted together. He not only had to know how to fire the gun but how to strip and re-assemble it under all types of conditions and circumstances, so his prior familiarity with machinery and metal components would have been extremely useful. He would also have had to exhibit the spirit detailed in the training manual which held that 'all machine gunners should be imbued with the determination to face any sacrifice in order to carry out their role in battle'. The manual also pointed out that the work of a machine gunner 'includes carrying weights, sometimes over long distances', so 'staying power is of great importance' when selecting men for this role. These special skills were later referred to by Lt Colonel GS Hutchinson in his 1937 book *Machine Guns – Their History and Tactical Employment*. Hutchinson considered that a machine-gunner required 'unusual strength of body and suppleness of muscles; the keen eye and cunning hand; speed of foot; steel nerves, a stout heart – these are the physical requirements. The machine gunner must be possessed, also, of intelligence above the average; his mind must be swift as a bullet in flight: he must be resourceful, audacious, possessed of initiative, and capable of endurance to the uttermost'.

From the 2nd May 1927, George's battalion was stationed at the Tower of London, having marched the five miles or so from Chelsea the day before. Although George and his comrades on the march were not wearing their Guard Order uniforms, they were wearing a uniform known as Change of Quarter Order. This consisted of khaki battledress jacket, and trousers with long puttees. They wore a large pack on the back with a small pack below, a water bottle on the right hip and a bayonet in its scabbard on the left, while the belt at the front held ammunition pouches. The bearskin caps worn on ceremonial duties had also been replaced by a forage cap with a white band, the use of which had led to the Coldstream Guards being nicknamed the Lilywhites. The whole outfit was, quite naturally in the Guards, all tightly buttoned, but it was the puttees that the guardsmen disliked the most. These were strips of cloth wound around each leg from ankle to knee and designed to protect and support the leg, but they were fiddly to put on correctly and very hot to wear. They were eventually replaced early in World War 2 by the more practical gaiters.

This particular uniform was, I suspect rather politely, described in the *Household Brigade Magazine* as 'not exactly the last word in comfort'. The article went on to describe the day of the march as 'the only hot day of this summer' and to say that the soldiers 'were very glad when the Tower came in sight after passing through the seaside smell of Billingsgate'. This reference to Billingsgate, of course, is to London's famous fish market, which was at that time located on the north bank of the Thames near to the Tower of London. I imagine that the 'seaside' smell of the fish must have been rather overpowering in the heat of the day to the weary guardsmen as they marched past the market on their way to the Tower.

I think it fascinating that these changes in garrison from one barracks to another were all accomplished on the march.

Those days before the introduction of motorised transport for the troops must have seen parts of the Capital echoing almost constantly to the sound of marching feet as units of the Guards marched from barracks to barracks, or from barracks to railway station and back again when they were stationed out of town. This constant marching to and fro calls to mind a paragraph from the Caterham Lecturers' Notes to the effect that Infantry soldiers must pay the greatest attention to their feet, 'as their whole utility depends on their marching power'.

Once at the Tower, the soldiers were housed in the Waterloo Barracks building. This had been constructed in 1846 on the site of the Grand Storehouse, which had burned down in 1841, and was built in a castellated neo-Gothic style close to the central White Tower. It was designed to house 1000 soldiers and continued to be occupied as such until 1956, when the Tower Garrison was withdrawn. By the time Shirley and I visited the Tower in 2006, it was being used to house the Crown Jewels.

Having been given time to settle into their new home, the battalion was inspected by the Regimental Lt Colonel on 23rd June while wearing their immaculate full ceremonial uniform. A report of this event noted that 'the many visitors to the Tower were afforded a grand sight'.

George had a break from garrison duties at the Tower in September when his Machine Gun Company was linked with that of the 1st Battalion Irish Guards and sent on a brigade training exercise along with the 1st and 3rd Battalions Grenadier Guards. The exercise was held near the Buckinghamshire /Oxfordshire border to the north of the town of Thame and is recorded as having taken place over '36 square miles of admirable training ground'. Although this event must have resulted in some considerable disruption to the local community, the soldiers found themselves welcomed not only by many former guardsmen living in the area but also by 'a great number of very hospitable squires and farmers'. During the 10 days the training exercise lasted, the troops 'stormed villages, crossed rivers at midnight, defended positions to the last gasp, and skillfully retired from others' before exchanging the fresh air of the countryside once more for the smokier environs of the Tower of London.

With so many men living in such close proximity in the Tower's barracks there was always the potential danger from disease, which was why the Army placed so much emphasis on health and personal cleanliness. However it did not always prove possible to ward off every disease, and towards the end of the year the battalion was apparently being 'handicapped' by an outbreak of diphtheria. This is a highly infectious disease of the throat, and the sufferers had to be isolated to prevent the spread of the disease. Nonetheless, the battalion was able to continue with its guard duties at the Tower as well as maintaining its winter training programme, although the lack of duty men did curtail its part in the Armistice Day celebrations.

The disease had seemingly barely died down before the battalion was called to action in response to a sudden and severe flooding of the Tower. This occurred on the night of the 6th - 7th January 1928 when, at about 1.30 am, a tidal wave swept over the wharf which separates the Tower from the River Thames and into the moat, filling it from end to end within ten minutes. This tidal wave also destroyed portions of the Moat's retaining wall, and the resultant floodwater filled the Byward Tower to a depth of four feet. The floodwater also washed away the sentry box from the wharf, flooded the Wharf and Spur guardrooms and washed away the road leading to the Jewel House. The water level then gradually dropped, but the formerly dry moat remained full of water for two or three days while the garrison was engaged in the dirty work of clearing up the flood's mess. There is also the story of an incident at the start of the flooding when an NCO rushed to the Tower's guardroom and 'strongly urged' the Sergeant of the Guard to ring for the Fire Brigade. The Sergeant however, not seeing any fire, and observing the rising flood, apparently formed the opinion that the Tower now had more than enough water of its own, so querulously exclaimed 'But why should I 'phone for the Fire Brigade?' The prompt and naturally rather agitated reply was that of course the firemen were needed 'to pump the water back into the Thames before the Tower is all under water!'

Shortly after this event, on the 25th February 1928, George married Evelyn Dobson at the Register Office in Nottingham. The marriage was witnessed by T. Hardy and W. Mitchell who, I imagine, were friends of the couple. I expect that George and Evelyn had met during one of George's trips to Nottingham on a visit to see Flo, or perhaps more likely to see his maternal grandmother; her Bateman Street address is in the same area of Nottingham as that of Evelyn, who then must have fallen for this tall and handsome Coldstream Guards Lance Corporal. Evelyn's address is shown on the marriage certificate as 8 Breedon's Buildings, Nuthall Road, where she is presumably living with her mother. Her father, William Dobson, a former 'Lace Merchant's Van Driver', had died some time previously. George's address is simply shown as 'Tower of London, London EC3.' It was apparently a hasty marriage, and I have been told that Lyn, at least, disapproved of George's new wife, so he must have noticed that George and Evelyn were not really suited to each other.

George was 24 when he married Evelyn, so he was too young to qualify for the provision of a married quarter or to receive any Married Soldier's Allowance. This must have made life quite difficult for them. The Standing Orders of the Coldstream Guards were very clear on this issue, stating that 'No soldier, regardless of rank, is eligible to be placed on the Married Quarters Roll until he is 26 years of age... Commanding Officers will explain to NCOs and Men who apply to get married under the age of 26 years that they are not entitled to be placed on the waiting list of the Married Quarters Roll, to be placed on the Marriage Allowance Roll, or to receive any special consideration until they have reached that age'. Evelyn therefore had to remain with her family in Nottingham while George returned to his duties at the Tower of London.

These duties were briefly interrupted on 2nd March when the battalion went to Pirbright Camp in Surrey for a seven-week training tour. This must have been a rather dismal experience, at least to start with, because it was noted that the day of the move was 'one of those days when we never see the sun'. Things apparently didn't get much better thereafter, because the report went on to state 'In fact, it rained incessantly for the first two days of our stay'. The report also noted 'There have been no great changes of scenery at Pirbright since last year and being the first Battalion to be stationed here this season, the camp was very gloomy in general. However, although the weather did its worst, Company and Battalion training was carried out successfully'.

Nonetheless the battalion's absence from London didn't diminish its ceremonial responsibilities, and it returned for the day on the 13th March to line the streets for a visit by King Amanullah, the King of Afghanistan, who was later forced into exile after a revolt in 1929. I do think that this task of 'street-lining' is such an important part of London's ceremonial occasions, with the guardsmen stationed at regular intervals along the road and standing in statue-like stillness before smartly presenting arms as the cavalcade passes. Sadly it can also be so often overlooked in the panoply of the procession.

The battalion subsequently returned to its Tower of London duties on 27th April.

Shortly after its return, the Battalion became involved in the rehearsals for the King's Birthday Parade which was to be held at the beginning of June, and for which the Household Brigade Magazine reported, in a delightfully old-fashioned turn of phrase, that the Battalion 'furnished Number 7 Guard'. The ceremony of Trooping the Colour was held each year on Horse Guards Parade and involved elements from all five Regiments of Foot Guards as well as the Royal Horse Guards, totalling some 2,000 troops in all together with six bands. It derives from the time when a regiment's colours, or flags, provided a rallying point in battle so it was important that every soldier was able to immediately recognise his regiment's colours. Accordingly they were 'trooped', or carried, along the ranks of soldiers each day. Only one colour can be trooped at a time, and the five Household Regiments therefore take it in turn each year. The colour being 'trooped' on this particular occasion was that of the Welsh Guards.

After the King had inspected the soldiers of both the Foot and the Horse Guards on the Parade Ground, and following a marching display by the Bands, the 'Escort to the Colour' from the Welsh Guards slowly trooped its Colour through the ranks of the assembled Foot Guards. The Guards then formed up and marched past the King in both slow and quick time, after which the Royal Horse Guards followed suit. The entire parade then escorted the King back to Buckingham Palace.

I think it almost certain that George would have taken part in this renowned ceremony and, if he did, I also think he could have been forgiven for finding his thoughts wandering and his concentration perhaps occasionally lapsing. This would have been only natural because, just over two months later on the 20th August 1928 at 119 Woodside Road Nottingham, he became a father when Evelyn gave birth to a son, Bernard. The property in Woodside Road was a council house on the Lenton Abbey Estate at the western edge of the City and had only recently been completed. The Nottingham Electoral Register for the city's Castle Ward, compiled on the 1st May 1929, shows that the house was occupied by three people - Alexander Measures, Gladys Measures and Evelyn Gaunt.

George's Army records also show Evelyn's address as being

in Nuthall Road during the time that she is described as his wife, so it seems probable that, after a short stay with her mother following the marriage, she then went to live with her sister and brother-in-law in Woodside Road ready for Bernard's birth. Here it was perhaps easier for George's sister Flo to provide help and support. It is also worth noting that these same Army records additionally show Evelyn's address at one point as being with Alfred Grimshaw at 270 Broad Lane Bramley. The records don't indicate the date of this particular event, but it may well have been in the early days of George's marriage when he was still too young to qualify for any married soldiers assistance from the Guards. Indeed, if Alfred did provide a home for Evelyn, even if only for a short time, it would certainly add support to the view that his relationship with George was perhaps closer than I had originally thought. However the Guards Regulations did require that George should 'immediately' report the fact of Bernard's birth to the Battalion's Orderly Room which, in turn, led to the formal announcement of the birth appearing in the Household Brigade Magazine: 'GAUNT. On August 20th 1928 to L/Sergt & Mrs Gaunt – a son Bernard Ronald.' For some reason, this announcement wasn't published until after George had subsequently been promoted.

One of the tasks required to be undertaken by the men comprising the Tower of London Garrison is the ceremony of 'The Keys.' This takes place each night at 9.50 pm, when an escort for the Tower's Keys consisting of one Sergeant, one Drummer and two Guardsmen parades under the Bloody Tower. The Guardsmen stand either side of the Chief Warder, who carries the keys to the Tower, with the Sergeant and the Drummer at the rear. After marching to the Barrier Gate, through the Middle Tower and the Byward Tower, locking each gate in turn, the Chief Warder and his Escort return to the Bloody Tower, where the Main Guard is waiting. The sentry at the Jewell House challenges with a loud 'Halt! Who comes there?' The Chief Warden replies 'The Keys'. 'Whose Keys?' the sentry asks. 'King George's Keys' responds the Warder. The sentry is then satisfied, 'Pass King George's Keys. All's well.' he calls out and then presents arms. The Chief Warder steps forward and says 'God preserve King George', and The Guard and Escort answer 'Amen.' This particular ceremony, which dates back to the 14th century, continues to be performed to this day.

The Bloody Tower is one of the more forbidding names at the Tower of London. It was originally called the Garden Tower before its modern name from the deadly events which occurred within its walls. This included the infamous 1483 murder of 'the princes in the tower', when the 12 year-old Prince Edward and his brother Richard were murdered and their bodies walled up inside the tower.

On the 1st October 1928 George's Annual Report showed that while still a Lance Corporal he was now a 'Machine Gun NCO', and his reporting officer praised the manner in which he had commanded his sub-section during manoeuvres. This is illuminating, because it seems to indicate that George had, at some point, undertaken the duties normally associated with a higher-ranked sergeant, who usually commanded the sub-section, and that he had performed well in that role. The report went on to say that he had 'developed into a very capable

NCO' and described him as being 'smart and hardworking with plenty of self-reliance'.

On the 4th October George and the battalion left the Tower of London and moved to Aldershot, where it was reported 'as soon as we had put our house in order the Brigadier Commanding 1st Guards Brigade descended upon us, carried out his annual inspection on December 5th and, as usual, warmed the battalion's heart with a very complimentary report.' Nevertheless I imagine that the warm glow of satisfaction and pride felt by George and the rest of the battalion at this event was probably short-lived, because they very quickly found themselves being called upon to undertake some onerous duties of a decidedly non-military nature.

The Brigade Magazine reported that, on the 10th December, the battalion 'commenced what was officially known as Digging and Constructional Work'. The article described the job with some feeling as 'gardening on a grand scale,' and invited interested parties to visit the Rushmoor Arena to 'view for themselves the accomplishment of the battalion during their week of toiling.' This work seems to me a rather odd task for an élite military unit, but obviously someone must have thought it a good idea. Rushmoor Arena is a grassed arena in the Hampshire countryside near Aldershot used to host various military tattoos. The reference in the magazine seems to relate to some reconstruction work that the battalion was called upon to undertake in preparation for the next event the following year.

However it was not all manual labour and military exercises. Sport, too, played an important part in the battalion's activities, because it was regarded by the Army as an essential element in helping to keep soldiers fit. Accordingly George was selected to play for the Battalion's rugby team during the 1928/29 season. The team's standard of play was regarded as having been 'highly satisfactory throughout the season' and the players were described as representing 'the best team the Battalion has organised for some years'. Playing in the Prince of Wales Rugby Cup, the team's 'first match of note' was in the 2nd Round against the Guards Depot who were beaten by 11 points to 7 'after a very hard but never the less a very clean game'. In the semi-final, the team encountered stiff opposition from the Royal Horse Guards, and after a 'thrilling game', passed into the final. Their opponents in this match were the 'doughty 1st Battalion Welsh Guards' who were to eventually win by 11 points to 7, so George and his team-mates had to console themselves with a Runners-Up Medal.

The latter part of January 1929 saw George's place in the machine gun platoon being cemented when he was sent on a rangefinding course at the Military College of Science in Woolwich. According to the Small Arms Training Manual, soldiers selected to be trained as range takers had to demonstrate that they were intelligent, that they possessed a 2nd Class Certificate of Education and that they had good eyesight. The course which George attended covered such elements as accuracy of range calculation, use of ground and cover and the care and cleaning of the instrument itself, which was cylindrical in shape, about 32 inches long and weighing just over 10lbs. It had centrally-mounted eyepieces and was set on a tripod stand. The skill of the range taker was to use this instrument to accurately estimate the distance to an object or a target. This was essential, firstly for the successful and safe deployment of the machine gun and its crew and secondly to ensure the safety of friendly troops, because of the considerable distances over which the gun could fire. George's pass mark for this course was graded as 'satisfactory'.

This year proved to be a particularly busy time for George, because his military duties and performances on the rugby field were supplemented by involvement in Athletics events. On the 31st May he took part in the battalion's Sports Meeting. This event was reported as being held in fine weather at the Guards Sports Ground watched by 'a good attendance of spectators' and was 'a notable success'. George was picked to represent his Company at two Championship events, coming 3rd in the One Mile Race and a creditable 2nd in the Three Mile Race. The Inter Company Championship was eventually won by Number 1 Company, with HQ Company coming 2nd and George's Company securing 3rd place.

George's army training continued throughout the year. His preliminary regimental instruction in respect of his duties as a machine gunner was brought to a conclusion by attendance at a formal machine gun training course during August and September. The course consisted of a series of indoor lectures and tests, supplemented by outdoor field firing exercises with the object of training the machine gunners so that 'whatever the conditions of ground or visibility, accurate and safe fire support can quickly be afforded to the rifle companies throughout all phases of the battle.'

The course was held at the Small Arms School at

Netheravon in Wiltshire, which is almost in the middle of the Army's Salisbury Plain Training Area and so was ideally situated for the necessary outdoor tactical training. George passed out top of the course and was awarded his Machine Gunner's Skill-at-Arms badge. The awarding of these badges was a well-tried and effective way for the Army to instill pride and competition in soldiers, and to make them feel superior to others. The success of this course was then crowned by another positive report on 3rd October, which recorded George's continuing role as 'Machine Gun NCO' and went on to note that he was 'very capable', being 'hardworking, reliable, intelligent and smart.' The report ended by stating that 'he gets a job done well by the men.'

The date of George's annual reports always seemed to herald a move by his battalion; and 1929 was no different because a move to the barracks at Chelsea came next and then, on the 10th October, the 1st XV Rugby Team, with George in the forwards pack, entered the Army Cup. They also entered the Prince of Wales' Rugby Cup, in which, of course, they had been the defeated finalists during the previous season. The team was entered into these competitions on a wave of enthusiasm reflected by the Brigade Magazine, which concluded that 'there is every chance of at least both of these cups swelling our collection of trophies'.

The first match in the Army Cup was against the 3rd Battalion Coldstream Guards on 2nd November 1929 at Hyde Park. The match report noted that it had 'proved a rare combat, and no side could score' so it went on to be decided at an eagerly-awaited return match. This replay was eventually won, after 'a very good game' by 11 points to 8. The report describing the rest of the competition noted that: 'For the second round we travelled to Woolwich and, after a very exciting and fast game, in which the issue was in doubt until the final whistle sounded, we beat the Military College of Science by 8 points to 6. Our next opponents were the 3rd Light Brigade Royal Artillery, and after 80 minutes wallowing and sliding in the mud, we survived, winning by 10 points to 3. And then, in the fourth round, came our exit. On 23rd January we gave battle to the Training Battalion Royal Engineers at Chatham. At full time neither side had been able to score, but during extra time the Royal Engineers scored two tries in quick succession, then we replied with an excellent try which was converted. Until the final whistle sounded there were many breathless moments, and though our team lost' by 5 points to 6, 'the display they gave was most creditable'.

Notwithstanding the importance attached to the training programme for these key rugby matches, it could not be allowed to impose on the needs of the service, so George was away from the training ground on Monday 2nd December when he undertook a Class of Instruction for promotion to Corporal, which he successfully passed. This was then followed by promotion to that rank on the 5th December, which led to his being appointed to the rank of Lance Sergeant on the 3rd January 1930. As noted earlier, this rank is peculiar to the Foot Guards, where all Corporals are appointed to Lance Sergeant although continuing to undertake the duties of a Corporal.

Meanwhile, on the sporting front, things got better for the rugby team in the Prince of Wales Cup at the end of January, when they beat the 1st Battalion Grenadier Guards by 34 points to nil. The team then went on to see off the Grenadier's 2nd Battalion by 27 points to 3 in the semi-final. This comprehensive win eventually pitted them against the Royal Horse Guards in the final, which they won by 10 points to nil, and so George at last received his Winner's Medal, which has been passed on to me. This victory made them the first Battalion team to win the Prince of Wales Cup, and the *Household Brigade Magazine* recorded its 'heartiest congratulations' on the event. The magazine, whose description of the competition they won was surprisingly shorter than the description of the loss of the Army Cup, concluded that 'The winning of the Prince of Wales Cup enables us to look back on last season with great satisfaction'.

George's sporting activities continued to include other events as well as rugby, and on the 7th April he competed in the battalion's Annual Cross Country Run. This was held over a course of about four miles at Pirbright Camp, and each Company in the Battalion entered a team of 30. These teams had been selected after what was described as 'some very competitive training, voluntary and involuntary before dawn and after dusk'. George was among them, again representing his Number 2 Company, and he came a strong second in the race. This occasion was quickly followed, on the 11th April, by the battalion sports meeting, held in fine weather which 'favoured a very successful meeting'. It was also noted that 'with better facilities for training at Pirbright, a heavy list of entries resulted and better results were obtained'. George once more represented Number 2 Company and improved on his place in the one-mile race, coming 2nd this time, while he repeated his 2nd place of the previous year in the three-mile race.

Hardly had the dust settled from these exertions than George was sent away to deepest Wiltshire, where he attended a Regimental Instructors' Course at the Porton Down Chemical Warfare School. This course lasted for the whole of May. Although I do not know the precise details, it is likely to have related to anti-gas defence, which the school was specializing in at the time. George finished the course with a Q2 qualifying mark.

The autumn of 1930 saw the battalion undergo a month's training at Pirbright in September, during which time George received his Annual Report. This recorded that he was now both a Machine Gunner and a Range Finder and described him as 'a very good NCO indeed' with 'a good manner', and in acknowledgement of his sporting activities, described him as 'a useful athlete.' The Pirbright training was followed by a few days at Chelsea and then, according to the Brigade Magazine, 'a quick move to Wellington Barracks' on the 9th October. George, however, missed these moves, because he was sent to the Army School of Physical Training at Aldershot to attend the 33rd Assistant Instructors' Course from the 17th September to the 18th December, where he was awarded a 2nd Class Certificate. The Certificate recorded that the subjects covered on the course 'included the rudiments of Boxing, Swimming, Bayonet Fencing, Wrestling (Army Style) and the Organisation of Games'. To obtain a second class award the candidate had to score between 60-74%, and George's score totaled 73.95%.

When he rejoined the battalion at Wellington Barracks, one of the public duties with which George was involved, other than Guard Mounting, was the provision of the Guard Picket for the Bank of England. Each evening, at 7 pm in summer and 6 pm in winter, one officer, one sergeant, two corporals, a drummer and twenty guardsmen mounted guard over the Guardroom, Front Hall, Bartholomew Lane Entrance, Bullion Yard and the Directors' Room at the Bank. They marched to the Bank from their Barracks via Horse Guards Arch, the Embankment and Queen Victoria Street. The Officer of the Guard was provided with a free dinner for himself and one gentleman guest while the other ranks each received gratuities. By about 1950 this amounted to two shillings (10p) for the sergeant, one shilling and sixpence (7½p) for the corporals and one shilling (5p) for the rest. Sometimes however the guard picket was provided from Chelsea Barracks. This drew criticism from one guardsman, who pointed out that this involved a much longer march to the Bank than from elsewhere and that 'you march at attention the whole way'. The provision of a guard picket at the Bank of England had started in 1780 but ceased in 1973.

Despite starting the season with high hopes of repeating their previous success in the Prince of Wales Cup, the battalion's rugby team only managed to reach the semi-finals this time. They started the competition in fine form, defeating the 2ⁿᵈ Battalion Coldstream Guards by 49 points to nil before securing a much narrower victory over the 1ˢᵗ Battalion Scots Guards, 8 points to nil. Unfortunately they were then soundly beaten 30 points to nil by the 2ⁿᵈ Battalion Welsh Guards, who were described as being 'in fine form.' This disappointing end to George's rugby season was however offset on the 31st May in the Battalion Sports Meeting at Pirbright Camp. On 'a day of good sport and bad weather' he was very successful, winning both the three-mile and one-mile races as well as coming second in the 880 yards race. Looking at his consistent results in these events, I think that long distance running must obviously have been his forte.

Throughout this very full and active period of 1929-1930 George had attended a number of significant courses of instruction, as well as achieving further promotion and representing the battalion at sporting events. His annual reports had been uniformly very positive and it seems that his abilities had been clearly identified by his superiors, leaving him marked out in their minds for even greater progression in the future. The sad footnote to this intense period of his life is that his immediate family does seem to have been placed very much in the background, although there was some good news, because, on 9th December 1929, George had at last been placed on the Marriage Allowance Roll. This act followed his qualification for the allowance by reason of age after his 26th birthday on the 3rd December that year.

CHAPTER THREE

AN OUTSTANDING NCO

'The backbone of the Army is the non-commissioned man' -
Rudyard Kipling

On the 4th September 1931, while stationed at Warley
Barracks, George received his Annual Report, which was
fulsome in its praise. It stated that he was 'an NCO of
outstanding ability in all directions' and further held that 'if he
sticks to the Army he should go far.' If the object of this report
was to persuade George to remain in the Guards, it certainly
worked, because a mere three weeks later, on the 25th
September, he was granted permission to extend his service to
complete a total of 12 years with the colours. The Barracks at
Warley were close to the town of Brentwood in Essex but they
were closed in 1959, and in 1964 the site became the UK
Headquarters of the Ford Motor Company.

The receipt of orders announcing the battalion's departure
on overseas service to the Sudan and Egypt must have come
as something of a two-edged sword for George. On the one
hand there was the sense of adventure inherent in travelling to

faraway places, but on the other hand this feeling must have been tempered by the knowledge that he would have to leave behind his six-months-pregnant wife and young son. Nevertheless, at the break of dawn on the 22nd March 1932, the battalion marched out of Warley Barracks to tread the 1½ miles or so to Brentwood railway station

The record of this event recalls that the soldiers sang 'traditional songs' as they marched, and that one of these was 'And remember that the best of friends must part', although this is in fact just a line from the old music hall song *There is a Tavern in the Town*. The rattle of the drums, the tramp of the marching feet and the singing of the soldiers must have brought a whole new meaning to the phrase 'dawn chorus' for the residents of Brentwood as the column wound its way to the station in the early light. Having boarded the train, the troops then travelled on to Liverpool, which they reached at about 2pm before embarking on the SS *Tuscania*.

The voyage south after they had reached sunnier climes has been described as the perfect cruise, with the men living 'in almost legendary comfort'; a far cry indeed from the strict barracks conditions they normally endured. Accommodated in two or four-man 2nd and 3rd class cabins, the soldiers had stewards to do all the cleaning, tidying and bed-making for them, while they were reported to have had 'plenty of time to enjoy the sun on deck, take part in Company sports and spend money at the well-equipped tuck shop'. Indeed the daily timetable concentrated as much on meals as it did on anything else: PT at 7 am for 20 minutes, breakfast at 7.30 am, general parade 10 am, dinners at 12 noon and 12.30 pm and teas at 5 and 5.30 pm, followed by supper at 9 pm.

As the *Tuscania* passed through the Straits of Gibraltar on Saturday the 26th March, George gained his first sight of the giant and impressive Rock of Gibraltar. Although he didn't know it at the time, he would be stationed there in the years ahead. Anchored briefly in Gibraltar Bay, the ship was soon surrounded by hawkers in rowing boats selling all kinds of goods. Unfortunately, as the soldiers soon discovered, many of these goods failed to match the prices originally paid for them and there was much grumbling from those who had been short-changed as the ship weighed anchor and steamed off into the Mediterranean. After a brief stop at Marseilles, the ship eventually arrived at Port Said on the 1st April, where, as at Gibraltar, it was again surrounded by hawkers in rowing boats. However the guardsmen were not to be hoodwinked a second time. According to reports, 'an enormous basket of offal of all sorts' was dropped on to the nearest hawkers, making them draw off 'with wild threats and curses'.

Passing through the Suez Canal during the night and on to the Red Sea, the *Tuscania* eventually reached Port Sudan at 6 pm on the 4th April, where the battalion disembarked before the ship then continued on its way to Bombay.

That same evening, after a meal taken aboard the crowded troopship *Dorsetshire* in the harbour, the battalion left the port in three separate trains. Battalion HQ, with No 1 Company and the majority of No 2 (MG) Company travelled to Khartoum North. No 4 Company went to Gebit, an isolated post in the Red Sea hills, while No 3 Company, together with a detached Platoon including George from the Machine Gun Company, journeyed to Atbara, a railway junction on the Nile about 170 miles north of Khartoum. They arrived at the town in the midday heat of the 5th April to find that their barracks were pleasantly situated on the banks of the Nile and surrounded by much vegetation.

The following couple of months were largely uneventful, although George did receive the welcome news that Evelyn had safely given birth to a daughter, Marion, on the 12th June 1932. Marion's birth certificate records that she was born at St John's, Redhill in Surrey, while Evelyn's address is shown as being 34 Beechen Lane, Lower Kingswood. This is about two miles north of Reigate, and the house, not being attached to any barracks complex, was probably a rented property. As with Bernard's earlier birth, an announcement duly appeared in the *Household Brigade Magazine*: 'GAUNT – To L/Sergt and Mrs G Gaunt – a daughter. Marion Grace'.

George's platoon was reunited with its parent company on the 7th July when No 2 (MG) Company arrived in Atbara to swop places with No 3 Company, which departed for Khartoum. The Company then commenced an extensive programme of practice shooting on the ranges three times each week. This routine lasted until the beginning of October and involved a two-mile march to the range, with the troops having to leave their barracks at 4.45 am. This allowed them to start the firing exercises at first light and finish before the heat of the day, which averages 35 degrees Centigrade (94 degrees Fahrenheit) in the summer, made the ranges unusable.

The Sudan had been generally peaceful since 1924, so the soldiers were not involved in any operational activity. Accordingly much of their time there was spent in various activities designed to help the troops cope with the primitive conditions in a tropical country at the start of the hot weather period. Apart from firing on the ranges and other military training, the soldiers were often engaged in extensive physical training, games and sports of every kind. This ensured that not only was sickness kept at bay, but that the fitness of the men actually improved. A particular advantage for the men stationed in Atbara was that they were allowed to use the swimming baths at the Atbara Sports Club. This proved very popular, and it was here that many of the men, including George on the 2nd August, were able to pass their swimming tests. Indeed it was subsequently reported that 'the non-swimmers roll became a thing of the past.'

In his confidential report for the 20th September, made towards the end of his stay in Atbara, George is described as 'an exceptionally good all round NCO'. It further noted that he was 'a good instructor and a good commander' and 'a good all round athlete'. The report also hinted at the direction of George's future employment when it noted that 'He has been employed as an acting Camp Quartermaster Sergeant at Atbara and has done the work very well'.

Their time in Atbara eventually came to an end and the Machine Gun Company left the town by train and rendezvoused with the rest of the battalion at Port Sudan before departing for Egypt on the 22nd October 1932. Travelling aboard the Troopship *Nevassa*, the guardsmen steamed north through the Red Sea before disembarking at Port Suez and then journeying for a few hours on the train to Cairo, which they reached on the 24th October. The Battalion was then based in the Kasr-el-Nil Barracks, where they relieved the 1st Battalion, Grenadier Guards. The barracks were located next to the River Nile and on the periphery of Cairo's European District. Kasr-el-Nil means 'Castle, or Fort, on the Nile' and, following demolition in 1947, it was replaced by Cairo's Nile Hilton Hotel and the nearby Central Bus Station.

Following an inspection by the commander of the Cairo Brigade on the 4th November, the battalion commenced an extensive training programme. This was carried out by each company in turn at Maadi, some eight miles out of Cairo, and lasted until the 23rd December. Next came a short break for Christmas, which was celebrated in style on the day with an open-air dinner reportedly followed by 'an inactive afternoon.' The happy day was rounded off by attendance at 'a 'Talkie' show in the Garrison Cinema during the evening.

There was a return to Maadi for battalion training from the 8th to the 22nd January 1933, by which time a writer in the *Household Brigade Magazine* noted that the soldiers 'were convinced that the Libyan Desert was part and parcel of the camp'. Even more sand was apparently encountered at Mena Camp where the battalion was based during the Brigade Training and the Egyptian Command Manoeuvres which commenced on the 24th February and continued into March. Mena camp was close to the Pyramids of Giza and to the Great Sphinx, which George and some of his friends were able to visit in their off-duty time. The training programme also took the battalion to a place called Saqqara, another site of great antiquity.

This round of military training for the battalion was

followed by its Sports Meeting, which was held in the grounds of the National Sporting Club on Cairo's Gezira Island on the 3rd and 4th April. A report of the occasion noted that 'some excellent sports were witnessed', and the meeting gave George the opportunity to participate in his favoured running events, where his performance was up to its usual standard. He won the one-mile race and came second in the 880 yards, but he also participated in two new events where he achieved some measure of success, coming 2nd in the pole vault and 3rd in the high jump.

The British Army in Egypt appears to have had the use of an armoured train, because the *Household Brigade Magazine* contains a fascinating, if all too brief, reference: 'The armoured train, which is allowed out once a year, proceeded to Alkam in June for a practice run and shoot.' The item goes on to say that the train 'was manned by personnel of No 2 Company', so George could easily have been one of those who took part in this exercise. An armoured train had armoured plate protecting the engine, the driver's cab and the wagons, which contained machine guns and carried troops. These trains were mainly used during the late 19th and early 20th centuries but were replaced over the years by more manoeuvrable road vehicles such as tanks and armoured cars.

A wind of change blew through the battalion on the 1st September 1933 when No 2 (Machine Gun) Company was retitled 'No 2 (Support) Company'. This change in name coincided with the replacement of one machine gun platoon in the company with a mortar platoon, although this was more a change in spirit than in fact because the new platoon hadn't been issued with any mortars. Indeed, the Brigade magazine commented that 'when the mortars will arrive is too much a hazard for a date or even a year to be fixed.'

The 1st September was also the date of George's annual report, in which he is characterized as 'a very steady and capable Sergeant'. The narrative also noted that he had 'recently become a Platoon Sergeant' which means that he would have been the most senior NCO in the platoon, working with the Platoon Commander. George's athletic prowess continued to be recognised as he was, once again, described as 'a good all round athlete'. His reporting officer closed the report with the comment that George is 'a very pleasant person to deal with.'

A noteworthy aspect of George's reports for the years from 1931 to 1933 is that his Company Commander during this time was Captain Arnold de L Cazenove, who went on become a brigadier. He had two sons, Christopher and Robert. Christopher Cazenove was an actor who came to prominence in an early 1970s military drama called *The Regiment*, in which he played an officer character intriguingly named 'Gaunt'. He went on to star in numerous films such as *Zulu Dawn* (1979) and *Eye of the Needle* (1981) as well as many television series such as *Dynasty* (1986–87) and *Judge John Deed* (2002-3). He died in 2010. Robert followed his father into the Coldstream Guards, rising to the rank of Major, and by some quirk of fate he was the person who responded to my letters when I wrote to the Coldstream HQ during my research for this book.

The Battalion eventually moved out of the Kasr-el-Nil barracks on the 27th November 1933 and travelled by overnight train to Alexandria, where it embarked once more on the Troopship *Nevassa*, but this time it was for the return passage to England. This voyage was acknowledged to be in 'strong contrast' to the battalion's much more comfortable outward journey in 1932. The ship seems to have encountered some particularly rough seas after sailing from Alexandria, and the *Household Brigade Magazine* noted that 'Mal de Mediterranean' turned the battalion's complexion to a pale white, changing slowly to sea-green'. However George had a reputation for being a good sailor, so he is likely to have been spared the seasickness which so affected some of his comrades.

The voyage to Gibraltar was portrayed as 'calm' while the often stormy Bay of Biscay was described as 'languid', although 'the last few hundred miles were passed in a frost of fourteen degrees' and the battalion landed at Southampton on the 9th December in bitter cold. 'Slow but sure trains' carried the soldiers to Brentwood station, and then came the march to their barracks at Warley which they reached later the same day.

George's posting to The Sudan and Egypt meant that he missed both marriages of his half-siblings, Flo and Lyn. The first to get married was Lyn, who by that time was living at 382 Broad Lane Bramley and working as a tailor's cutter. He married Elsie Briggs on the 15th April 1933 at St Peter's Church in Bramley. Flo, meanwhile, was working in Nottingham as a machinist of fancy linen and living with the Hartshorn family at a property called The Rosemary in Newstead Avenue, Westdale Lane, Carlton. She got married later that year, on the 23rd December, in Nottingham's Basford Register Office, to Walter Ross, a Scotsman whose work as a journeyman joiner had brought him to the city from Edinburgh. Walter's address on the marriage certificate is also shown as The Rosemary, so he was presumably lodging at the house where he and Flo must have met. Witnesses to the marriage were Frank and Ivy Hartshorn. Missing these important events must have been especially sad for George because he, Flo and Lyn were so close. This closeness would last throughout their lives, and when together, they always had at least one session of intense private talks. I have been told that spouses were never excluded from these talks but they rarely, if ever, participated.

The battalion's return from Egypt was followed by a very welcome six weeks' leave' which gave George the opportunity to see his 18 month-old daughter, Marion, for the first time. It could also have been about this time that Evelyn and the children moved from Surrey, where they were living when Marion was born, to be closer to George at Warley Barracks. Bernard was five years old by now and one of his earliest memories is of living in Brentwood; George's service documents do show an address for his family in Warley Hill, Brentwood. The period of leave was then followed by preparations for a transfer down the road to London's West End. This took place on the 9th April when the battalion moved into Wellington Barracks, to become engaged in a hectic round of ceremonial activity.

In addition to the usual duties such as Guard Mounting they were called upon to provide a guard of honour for a Court at Buckingham Palace and for the King at the opening of the Royal Tournament, and then to provide detachments for

Numbers 7 and 8 Guards, together with soldiers, to line the route for the King's Birthday Parade in June. All of this activity of course necessitated considerable practice and rehearsal to ensure that nothing could possibly go wrong. This was followed on the 5th June by a move to Pirbright Camp for weapon training in what the magazine described as 'almost tropical weather' before a very busy period which concluded with a final move to the Tower of London on the 3rd July 1934.

The Battalion's stay at the Tower was relatively short, lasting only until September, when it was transferred to Aldershot. It was here that George received the news that Alfred Grimshaw had died on the 21st September at 3 Green Hill Road Armley, on the outskirts of Leeds. This was presumably the address of a relative, because Alfred's home address is listed on the death certificate as Broad Lane in Bramley, albeit at number 388 (which still exists) rather than number 270 where Annie had died and which was demolished in the 1960s. Alfred is described on the death certificate as having been an 'Engineer (Dye Works)', although, according to Lyn's April 1933 marriage certificate, he had retired by that time. I imagine his change of job may have been prompted by a need to seek something less arduous than working in a foundry. He could therefore have readily worked in the Aire Vale Dye works, about a mile or so from his house in Broad Lane. His funeral was held at the Farsley Rehoboth Particular Chapel on the 25th September.

With Flo now living in Nottingham, George's only contact with Yorkshire remained Lyn, who was still living in Bramley before his eventual move across the Pennines to Manchester. I can find no history of George having any contact with other relatives of his father, despite Alfred Gaunt having been survived by two younger brothers (William and Herbert). However they had both moved away to Cleckheaton. With both of them also having young families, it is entirely possible that they simply drifted apart from the son of their older brother.

George's report for 1934 echoed the sentiments of his previous year's report by noting that he was still 'a very nice man to have anything to do with' and 'a capable sergeant, hardworking and reliable.' There was also a repeat of the reference to his sporting abilities, when he was again said to be 'a good all round athlete.' Shortly thereafter he was sent on a Long Qualifying Course in the Rifle and in the Light Automatic Gun held at the Small Arms School at Hythe in Kent. This lasted from the 15th October to the 21st December 1934, and he gained another good result, qualifying 'Q2'.

At some point around this time George was sent on a temporary detachment to the Guards Depot at Caterham, where he had undergone his initial Coldstream Guards training. He still hadn't qualified to be allocated a married quarter, so he had to live with Evelyn, Bernard and Marion in a rented bungalow in the town. The address of the bungalow is shown on his Military History Sheet as being in 'Honey Road' although I can't find that name on any modern street listing. Bernard did however recall that the school which he had to attend was inside the barrack complex. He later returned to Caterham as an 18 year-old Coldstream Guards recruit in 1946 and found that the conditions were just the same as they had been when his Dad had first been there nearly twenty years previously.

George's career in the Guards must have continued to

progress, because he was next promoted to the rank of Sergeant on the 17th April 1935 followed, on the 26th June at Aldershot, by his re-engagement in the Coldstream Guards for 'such term as shall complete 21 years service'. However he must have experienced some early difficulties after this promotion because the lieutenant writing his September 1935 report, although acknowledging that he was 'a smart hardworking NCO who has shown keenness', went on to criticise him for 'being unable to teach recruits drill mainly through the feebleness of his word of command'. Obviously this officer felt that George wasn't shouting at the recruits loudly enough.

On the 20th September 1935, after an absence of twelve years, the battalion moved to Windsor, the troops being transported by train from Basingstoke. George then sat and passed the final element of his 1st Class Army Certificate of Education, which was issued on the 16th October. The certificate listed the subjects covered as English, Mathematics, Geography and Map Reading, representing the culmination of a series of individual exams. He had passed the English and Map Reading element of the exam on the 20th March 1929, having achieved a distinction in Map Reading with a pass mark of 80%. He had then passed the Maths element on the 12th October 1932.

During the time George was stationed in Windsor, he and his family were able to live in a married quarter, because, on the 17th April 1935 and some six and a half years after his marriage, he had at long last been placed on the Married Quarters Roll. The house which had been allocated to him was inside the Guard's Victoria Barracks complex in Windsor's Sheet Street. Although this was in a most convenient location, the property had to be ready for inspection by the army authorities at any time during the day. This meant it always had to be kept presentable, just in case an inspection should be called at short notice.

George also had to be very much aware of a strict rule in the Regiment's Standing Orders that 'Soldiers on the Married Quarters Roll will be responsible to the Commanding Officer for the behaviour of their families'. Many years later when Bernard and Jo visited Windsor, they passed the Barracks and Bernard was able to see his old home still there, next to the piquet gate. However, when Shirley and I visited Windsor in 2011, our attempts to view the barracks were defeated by the high brick walls and gates, not to mention a rather formidable-looking armed sentry.

One of Bernard's chores at this time was to visit the barracks cookhouse once a week to collect the family's ration of meat, bread and tea. He was also often required to run errands for the wife of the Battalion's Regimental Sergeant Major. This was RSM Ronald Brittain, an archetypical RSM who was a famous personality in the Guards. He was an imposing figure of a man at six feet three inches tall, and had a fearsome reputation as well as, reputedly, the loudest voice in the British Army. I suspect that it was under his guidance that George learned how to project his voice so effectively and to develop his 'word of command'.

At one point Bernard recalled that the RSM put George under close arrest, although the nature of the offence is not known and no record was kept of the event. I think it must have been a comparatively minor offence because it certainly didn't harm George's career. However his Annual Report for the period ending in August 1936 does contain a slightly mysterious and somewhat obscure reference to some sort of happening. Having acknowledged that George was 'a smart and hardworking NCO who always does his best', the report cautioned that he 'should try and not get too excited when work presses or something unusual occurs'. Sadly that is as near as I could get to the detail of this particular matter.

RSM Brittain retired from the Army in 1954, and subsequently appeared in a variety of films, often as a Sergeant Major. They included *55 Days in Peking* (1963) and *Casino Royale* (1967). Ronald Brittain died in 1981.

Living in the barracks also gave Bernard many opportunities to watch, in wide-eyed fascination, as the Castle Guards prepared for and carried out their ceremonial duties, and as a seven-year old he particularly loved to follow in the footsteps of the Guards band when it paraded around the town and castle. Nonetheless, there was a serious side to Bernard's life in the barracks and, in addition to attendance at day school, George also made him attend the local Methodist Sunday school, emulating his own experience of being sent to a Methodist Sunday school when he was a child in Bramley. Bernard was also required to look after his younger sister and has a vivid recollection of an incident when he was playing with a group of boys while Marion played separately nearby with a group of girls. His father observed this situation and concluded that Bernard was not keeping a proper lookout for Marion, so he took him home and gave him a beating for this 'disobedience'. I think it extremely sad that, just as in this particular case, so many of Bernard's childhood memories are unpleasant rather than happy or joyful.

King George V died on the 20th January 1936 at the royal residence of Sandringham and, following the lying in state in London, his funeral was held at Windsor Castle on the 28th. As part of the Windsor garrison, George was involved in the extensive ceremonial which accompanied the funeral, his battalion providing two guards of honour - the first at the GWR station and the second in the Windsor Castle cloisters. Another detachment from the battalion formed part of the troops lining the streets from the station to the castle, which Bernard remembered in particular because he was sat on the edge of the pavement at the time watching between the soldiers' legs as the cortege passed by.

King George was succeeded by Edward VIII, who also became Colonel in Chief of the Coldstream Guards, and an early function of his brief reign was an inspection of the 1st Battalion at Windsor on the 24th April. This was described as 'a very memorable and happy occasion' where George was one of those taking part in the march past. Barely had the dust settled from this event before George's company was ordered to Wellington Barracks for three days on the 26th April to undertake ceremonial duties, in the absence of soldiers from the 2nd Battalion who had been sent away on a weapon training course. Then, as the 1st Battalion reassembled at the beginning of May, they reportedly became 'partly mechanized' with the issue of 18 trucks, two Austin Seven motor cars and two motor cycles. The trucks are likely to have been replacements for the horse-drawn wagons which had previously been used to transport the Support Company's equipment. However the vehicles were beset with mechanical problems, and two of the trucks and one Austin were soon out of commission. This prompted a writer in the *Household Brigade Magazine* to predict with some cynicism that with care, the motor transport should last 'until well into the middle of August.'

The ceremonial associated with the short-lived succession of Edward VIII to the throne probably reached its peak with his presentation of new colours to a total of six battalions of troops from the Brigade of Guards. This was undertaken at a huge ceremony in Hyde Park on the 16th July, when all three battalions of the Coldstream Guards, together with battalions from the Grenadier and Scots Guards, received their Colours from the King. At the conclusion of the ceremony, he rode back to Buckingham Palace at the head of his troops who, with George again marching amongst them, followed four abreast with their new colours proudly flying in a long colourful procession.

Shortly afterwards the battalion returned to London, where they were stationed at Wellington Barracks for the usual summer ceremonial season, which was due to be followed by a large-scale training programme. However this was interrupted on the 3rd September with news that troops were to be despatched to Palestine in order to help quell a dangerous armed uprising. The battalion was then ordered to move immediately to Windsor, where the men were informed that the 3rd Battalion Coldstream Guards were to form part of the Palestine-bound force. The author of George's previous report from the 1st Battalion had written that he had done 'extremely well' and could 'turn his hand to anything,' ending with the considerable endorsement that George was 'one of the best NCOs in the Battalion.' Therefore it probably came as no surprise that George was one of two experienced Sergeants, along with two officers and about 100 other ranks, who formed a draft of men sent to bolster the 3rd Battalion before its departure.

After what the *Household Brigade Magazine* next described as 'a hectic week-end,' these reinforcements marched out of Windsor on Monday 7th September bound for Aldershot, where they joined the 3rd Battalion, and where George was allocated a married quarter for his family. The soldier's arrival at Aldershot was then followed by a round of 'inoculations, vaccinations and clothing inspections' in preparation for their departure. Mustering a total of 28 officers and 663 other ranks, the 3rd Battalion finally embarked from Southampton on the 3rd October 1936 aboard the SS *Laurentic* of the Cunard White Star Line. The magazine's complimentary but somewhat land-lubberly description of the ship was 'as nice a boat as one could wish to see'.

Although the Guards were (indeed, still are) very highly trained élite soldiers, the arrival of orders sending them into action must have created a natural concern for them from their comrades in arms. This undercurrent of concern was revealed in the magazine's reporting of the troops' despatch, the articles being written by serving soldiers. It manifested itself not only in one writer wishing the 3rd battalion God speed and a short stay in the Holy Land but also in the fact that a large party from the 1st battalion travelled by road from Windsor to Southampton to give their comrades a 'heartening send-off to the music of the Regimental Band'. These well-wishers also received from the 3rd battalion 'a final Coldstream Cheer from the middle of Southampton Water'. The 3rd battalion was then reported as being 'outward bound and it was au revoir to old England for a while'.

Experiencing nothing more than a moderate swell in the English Channel and the Bay of Biscay, the ship passed Gibraltar at 10pm on the 6th October and entered the Mediterranean under sunny skies, the chief distractions for the troops being 'physical training, lectures and deck games' albeit overlaid with some apprehension about what they might face on arrival in Palestine. Malta was reached on Friday 9th October, when the *Laurentic* stopped, apparently 'for exactly five minutes,' to drop off the mail. The ship steamed close to the shore after it had weighed anchor and all the men were able to get a good view of the island, the magazine further reporting that 'the barracks and married quarters by the water's edge looked very attractive in the sunshine'. The south coast of Crete was passed the following day and their destination, the port of Haifa, was sighted at 5 am on Monday the 12th October.

The *Laurentic* docked in Haifa's 'wonderful natural harbour' shortly after breakfast and the troops disembarked at 1.30 pm. The magazine then reported that, having assembled in the dock area, the battalion was soon 'swinging along through the town, the inhabitants of which had turned out in full force' to see the soldiers marching with flags flying and 'to the stirring music of Drum-Major Tinsley'. Skirting the seashore in the afternoon sun, the battalion reached its rest camp, where it was to spend the night some three miles from the town. After a night under canvas, when the men encountered some 'weird and wonderful' insects, the battalion boarded a train at 6 am on an adjacent railway line and headed for Jerusalem. The journey along a twisting and curving track with some 'incredible gradients' was uneventful, and the city was reached at about noon.

Having arrived in Jerusalem, the battalion was quartered in the Kaizerein Augusta Hospice on the Mount of Olives. This was described as a 'beautifully built German structure' having been constructed in 1907 and named after the wife of Kaiser Wilhelm the II (it is still there today and is now known as the Augusta Victoria Hospital). The hospice had been seriously damaged during an earthquake in 1927, but had been repaired sufficiently to provide a home for the troops. However there was now nothing for them to do. The violence had blown over, at least for the time being, and the concerns of the soldiers' comrades back in England had been proved to be thankfully unfounded.

Accordingly, instead of confronting armed rebels, the men found themselves whiling away the hours with whist drives, concerts and other indoor amusements, or being taken on conducted tours to visit places of Biblical interest in and around Jerusalem such as the Holy Sepulchre, the Temple Area and the Garden of Gethsemane. There were also visits to other Holy Places such as Bethlehem. Indeed, so relaxed did this posting turn out to be that it became widely known as 'The Cooks Tour,' after the Thomas Cook Holiday Company. This 'rather monotonous routine' of life in the Holy Land ended with the news that the battalion was returning to England, and it was with 'glad hearts' that they sailed from Haifa on the 20th December, although this did mean that the soldiers celebrated Christmas aboard ship rather than at home with their families.

The ship eventually docked at Southampton on the 29th December, and the following day the troops travelled to Aldershot, so George was at least able to be with Evelyn, Bernard and Marion in time for the New Year.

On the 15th March 1937 George was posted to the Coldstream Guards Regimental Staff, where he was assigned the job of Recruiting Sergeant. The 1933 edition of the Standing Orders for the Coldstream Regiment of Foot Guards provided for two such sergeants to be attached to the Regimental Staff. George was then based in Hull, which was one of the regiment's recruiting locations. George's departure from the 3rd Battalion was marked by the presentation of a silver tankard which is now in my possession. It is inscribed with the Coldstream Guards crest and the wording 'Sergeants Mess 3rd Bn Coldstream Guards. G. Gaunt.'

George was as good at this job as he had been with previous roles, and after only six months the Officer in Charge of the Recruiting Office wrote in a confidential report that George 'has proved a good recruiting agent' and that he was 'very tactful in handling the nervous applicant'. The report closed with the comment that he was 'an intelligent, self-reliant and industrious NCO'. The job in Hull had removed George from the Guards' Public Duties in London, so he took no part in the Coronation ceremonial for King George VI on the 12th May 1937.

The posting to Yorkshire meant yet another move for the family, and Bernard told me he remembered the family moving from their married quarter in Aldershot to a rented house in Hull, where he attended the local school. The house he remembered must have either been in Rutland Road or Westlands Road, because both these addresses are shown on George's next of kin details in his personal documents.

In the summer of 1939, Bernard passed the entrance exam to attend Kingston upon Hull Grammar School but, as was so often the case, he was destined to be there for only a very short time. This was because George was promoted to Colour Sergeant (CQMS) on the 1st September 1939, followed, on the 2nd September, by a recall from Hull and posting to the Regiment's Training Battalion, which was then being established at Pirbright. A final report from his CO in Hull noted that George had 'worked very well' and was both conscientious and trustworthy.

The formal declaration of World War Two came on the 3rd September, and the Battalion's flurry of activity in preparation for that war was interrupted two days later, when George was detailed to provide the ceremonial guard during a formal visit and inspection of the Battalion by Field Marshall His Royal Highness Prince Arthur, Duke of Connaught. The Prince was a Great Uncle to King George VI, who also came to visit the Battalion, just over a week later on the 12th September.

The Coldstream Guard's Training Battalion, along with

that of the other Guards Regiments, had been established for the continuation of recruit training once the recruits had passed out of the Guards Depot at Caterham, and this new posting for George again resulted in a move for Evelyn, Bernard and Marion. They moved to live once more at Lower Kingswood in Surrey, where Bernard and Marion attended the local school. However a further move to a rented house in St Johns on the outskirts of Woking resulted in yet another change of schools for them both.

The Battalion's accommodation at Pirbright during the first part of September was not really sufficient for the numbers of troops being assembled there, so garages and other outbuildings had to be hurriedly utilised to house the newly-arrived soldiers. Neither was the situation helped by the poor weather. The rain and wind made life very difficult, particularly for those living under canvas, and George must have considered himself very fortunate to have been allocated a married quarter. However the situation for the battalion was eased somewhat when the 7th Guards Brigade departed for France, the *Household Brigade Magazine* reporting that they were given 'a hearty send-off' when they left. Despite the rigours of wartime training, the battalion didn't entirely abandon its off-duty moments and it was further reported that there was 'a number of exceptionally good concerts' with the dining-hall being packed to capacity on each occasion.

Sport also continued to play an important part in the battalion's life, and sub-committees were quickly established to organise various sporting activities. George appears to have moved on from his previous sports of rugby and long-distance running, because he is reported as now being in charge of the boxing sub-committee, which apparently could be 'relied upon to produce some good boxing teams from the large amount of talent available.'

On the 1st December George was promoted to Acting Warrant Officer II (Company Sergeant Major) as the battalion continued to expand, growing from its original four companies to a total of ten by the end of the month. The new arrivals included more than 700 reservists previously serving in organisations such as the police force and fire service. The age and experience of these men must also have required a slightly different approach to their training, compared to that of the younger recruits who had formed the bulk of the battalion's strength until now. Apart from coping with this mass of willing, and possibly not so willing, recruits, the weather continued to make life onerous for everyone.

The winter of 1939/40 was the most severe in living memory. January turned out to be the coldest month for many years, with heavy falls of snow and thick frosts. These Arctic weather conditions were reported to have brought the training programme more or less to a standstill, and all ranks, including George and the other senior NCOs, were employed in clearing the snow. Even the RSM 'was seen wielding a broom and shovel to great effect.' By this time a number of drafts had been sent on to the 1st 2nd and 3rd Coldstream battalions, but, with a steady flow of recruits from the Guards Depot, the strength of the Training Battalion still numbered well over 2,300 men.

The 1st March 1940 saw George's acting promotion being made substantive and his Medical Category listed as A1. The units at the camp were reorganised at the same time and he was now attached to Number 3 Company under Captain Burges. Training continued apace, and after the Dunkirk evacuation in May/June it included preparations for the battalion to be quickly deployed in response to the German invasion which was anticipated almost daily. Under these circumstances the initial training at the Guards Depot will have paid dividends, because the soldiers had been trained to always have all their equipment 'perfectly ready in case of having to turn out suddenly.'

Fortunately the invasion never came, although the training programme was regularly interrupted by air-raid alerts during that long summer of 1940 while the Battle of Britain raged overhead. However the tension of that time was eased with various social activities; every week the Sergeants Mess held well-attended song and dance social evenings, which resulted in a report that the Mess was 'now on a sound financial basis, largely due to the efforts of CSMs Kirkham and Gaunt and their Committees'. I think that achieving this healthy state of affairs was undoubtedly helped by the useful experience George gained during his time as acting camp quartermaster sergeant in Atbara.

George's role on the boxing sub-committee was not simply organizational because he actually took part in a number of competitions. The first major event took place on 27th November when the Coldstream Guards took on the Scots Guards in a tournament which is reported as having given 'an evening's first class entertainment to the large numbers who crowded the Camp theatre.' The meeting opened heavily for the Scots Guards challengers, who lost both lightweight bouts before they gained their first victory at the welterweight level. However this victory was 'nullified by CSM Gaunt defeating L/Sgt Harris in a very good fight.' The Coldstream Guards then went on to win the tournament by 17 points to the Scots Guards 16 points.

The next boxing event of note took place on the 22nd January 1941, when the Grenadier Guards Training Battalion sent over a team of thirteen to take on the Coldstream champions. Unfortunately the reporting of this event was very much limited by space restrictions, which simply recorded that amongst the winners was CSM Gaunt, who defeated L/Cpl Howorth in the welterweight competition. The Coldstream Guards saw off their challengers, winning the overall competition by 7 fights to 6.

One of George's last jobs with the Coldstream Guards was to form part of the detachment guarding the deputy German leader Rudolf Hess, who had had stolen a fighter plane and flown to Scotland on the 10th May 1941 in a doomed attempt to engineer a peace deal between Britain and Germany. After being captured by the Home Guard, Hess was initially held at Maryhill Barracks in Glasgow while the Government decided what to do with him. At a War Cabinet meeting on the 15th May it was agreed that he should be kept in isolation. Accordingly he was first brought to London by train on the 16th May escorted by a detachment of Scottish troops and temporarily held in the Queens House at the Tower of London, where he became one of the Tower's last prisoners.

Hess was then secretly moved on the 20th May to Mytchett Place, a run-down Victorian Mansion near Aldershot in Hampshire, known as 'Camp Z'. Once there he was guarded by detachments of both the Coldstream and Scots Guards taken from the nearby Guards Training Battalions at Pirbright Barracks and placed under the command of Lt Colonel A M Scott of the Scots Guards. Unfortunately the records relating to those soldiers who were sent to guard Hess are extremely limited. The Training Battalion didn't keep a War Diary, and while the Camp Diary kept by Lt Colonel Scott lists the officers at Mytchett Place, it only makes passing reference to a few of the other ranks. Accordingly there is no comprehensive central listing of exactly who was allocated to the task. However Bernard told me that George's participation was the subject of much discussion in the family, and I think George's rank and experience would have made it logical for him to have been involved in some way, although I don't know his precise role.

The authorities were particularly concerned that the Germans might attempt to rescue Hess or that there might be an assassination attempt, so Mytchett Place had been specially prepared for his arrival and was surrounded with barbed-wire fences, fixed trip-wires and camouflaged machine-gun emplacements. The decision to move Hess to Mytchett Place had been taken so quickly that the last of the workmen preparing the house had only just left before Hess and his escort from the Tower arrived. Hess remained at Mytchett Place until June 1942, when he was transferred to a former hospital near Abergavenny in Wales. In 1945 he was tried and convicted as a war criminal, and he spent the rest of his life in Spandau Prison, Berlin. He died in 1987.

CHAPTER FOUR

AIRBORNE FORCES

*'What manner of men are these who wear the maroon red beret?
They are firstly, <u>all</u> volunteers, and are then toughened by hard
physical training. As a result they have that infectious optimism and
that offensive eagerness which comes from physical well being. They
have 'jumped' from the air and by so doing have conquered fear.
Their duty lies in the van of battle; they are proud of this honour
and have never failed any task. They have the highest standards in
all things, whether it be skill in battle or smartness in the execution
of all peacetime duties.
They have shown themselves to be as tenacious and determined in
defence as they are courageous in attack. They are, in fact, men
apart - every man an Emperor.'*

- Field Marshall Viscount Montgomery of Alamein, 1950.

Britain's Airborne Forces were formed in mid-1940 when
Prime Minister Winston Churchill made his famous call for
the formation of 'a corps of at least five thousand parachute
troops'. The Commandos were also being created at this time,

and the decision was made to convert No 2 Commando to a parachute unit, being re-named 11th Special Air Service Battalion in November 1940 and, after that, 1st Parachute Battalion in early 1941. The subsequent formation of 2nd and 3rd Parachute Battalions then led to the creation of 1st Parachute Brigade, although this achievement fell some way short of the Prime Minister's initial ambition. In these early days of parachuting in the Army, the titles 'Special Air Service' and 'Parachute' were interchangeable; indeed, George's Military History Sheet shows his posting to India as being to 'SAS Bn India'.

At about the same time, in a telegram to officials in India dated the 17th June 1941, the Government approved in principle 'the formation of an airborne brigade in India subject to one battalion of the brigade being British.' During that same month George was successfully interviewed in London by Major (later Lt Colonel) Martin Lindsay and selected from other candidates to be eventually promoted as the first Warrant Officer I (Regimental Sergeant Major) of this new battalion, which was to be known as 151 (British) Parachute Battalion, 50 Parachute Brigade. The other two units in the Brigade were 152 (Indian) Parachute Battalion and 153 (Gurkha) Parachute Battalion. Martin Lindsay had been a polar explorer before the war, having been a member of the British Arctic Air Route Expedition in 1930-31 and then leading the British Trans-Greenland Expedition in 1934. He had also previously served in the Royal Scots Fusiliers before becoming a pioneer of parachuting, and was among the first six Army parachutists taking part in the early experimental parachute jumps during 1940.

George was then sent for parachute training to Ringway Aerodrome. This is now better known as Manchester Airport, and a small memorial garden alongside the ramp to Terminal 1 contains various Airborne Forces Memorials. He arrived on the 12th July and was met at Wilmslow Station by Lieutenant Peter Law of the Royal Ulster Rifles. Lt Law was also part of the draft due for India. Once at Ringway, George underwent a second interview with Major Lindsay and another with Lt Colonel John Rock, formerly of the Royal Engineers. Lt Col Rock was closely involved with the establishment of Airborne Forces in the UK, and was the first commander of the Glider Pilot Regiment, but he was killed in a training accident near the village of Shrewton on Salisbury Plain in 1942.

The training course was successfully completed, with George undertaking the required number of jumps to become a qualified parachutist and gaining his Parachute Qualification Wings (the much coveted paratroopers 'jump wings') on the 14th July. At 37 years of age, he was one of the older soldiers to qualify as a paratrooper, and his success in this endeavour clearly disproved the theory of the Army's Assistant Director of Medical Services who had claimed that men over the age of 30 could not support the rigours of being a paratrooper.

Unfortunately, this being in the very early days of the Airborne Forces, the records of his parachute training have not been retained, but it is likely that it will have involved jumping from an aeroplane, probably a converted bomber such as the Armstrong Whitworth Whitley, as well as a static balloon. The use of these balloons had been introduced in April 1941 only a couple of months before George arrived, and by late 1941 their use had been fully incorporated into the training programme.

The ideal scenario for the programme was that trainees completed two balloon jumps and five descents from an aircraft during their fourteen days of parachute training. However, jumping from an aeroplane could lead to the jumper somersaulting or twisting as he was caught in the aeroplane's slipstream, so this difficulty was virtually eliminated by the use of the balloon. Unfortunately the absence of slipstream gave no boost of wind to the filling of the parachute, which meant that it took longer to open fully open, and by the time it did the jumper was getting perilously close to the ground. Nonetheless, the Training Manual remained unmoved by any fears that such a situation may provoke, taking the view that the delayed opening of the parachute 'produces an additional thrill'. This was probably a thrill which many trainees could have done without, the balloon being described with some feeling at one point as a 'foul loathsome sausage'.

After a period of embarkation leave that followed the completion of his training programme, George sailed from Liverpool on the 30th August 1941 aboard the troop ship *Georgic*. Accompanying him were Lt Law and eight NCOs comprising the party chosen to train the parachutists in India. These were Quartermaster Sergeant Instructor J McNary and Sgt Corser (Army Physical Training Corps), Sgt Honeybun (The Buffs - Royal East Kent Regiment), Sgt Fritchley (The South Staffordshire Regiment), Sgt Smith (The Suffolk Regiment) Bombardiers Harden and Schofield (Royal Artillery) and Cpl Len Shepherd, who had been seconded to the RAF as a Parachute Jump Instructor. The convoy eventually docked at Bombay on the 24th of October and, on the 25th, the effective date of his acting promotion to RSM, George travelled on to Delhi, leaving the rest of the party to follow on the next day. Upon arrival at Delhi Railway Station he was met by RQMS J Murray and CSM J Bunch, and then reported to Lt Col Lindsay.

During the previous month the Lt Colonel had been busily touring India seeking out and interviewing the various volunteers for parachuting. After two years of war, many of the soldiers stationed in India still found themselves sidelined and undertaking simple garrison duties, so the formation of a parachute battalion offered them a great opportunity to become more directly involved in the fighting. Accordingly the response to the search for volunteers was overwhelming, although becoming a paratrooper was not at all easy: In one unit alone no fewer than 15 officers and over 300 men had volunteered, but only two officers and 70 men were able to pass the rigorous selection process. This consisted of an interview followed by a medical test, which was the same as that for RAF crew. Although this was later changed, it included a colour blindness test which alone resulted in some 20% of applicants being failed. The Parachute Battalion had been allocated barracks in Delhi cantonment recently vacated by the Duke of Wellington's Regiment and, following George's arrival, the successful volunteers began to report there for duty.

151 (British) Parachute Battalion was officially formed on the 15th October 1941, becoming the fourth parachute battalion in order of seniority. From the end of that month

until December 1941 trainees continued to join the battalion and, by January 1942, it was organised into five companies together with an additional first reinforcement company. This effort was a considerable achievement, because the battalion had to start forming from scratch, with men volunteering from all twenty seven infantry battalions stationed in India. There was not even a nucleus for the formation so, while successful volunteers were joining, indents were being rushed through for the arms and equipment necessary for equipping and training a normal infantry battalion. However, matters were eased somewhat by the fact that the newly-arrived officers and senior NCOs were experienced regular soldiers rather than raw recruits, so were better able to cope with the situation in which they found themselves. One of these officers was Captain Geoffrey Powell of the Green Howards, who would later distinguish himself in the fighting at Arnhem and then write a book entitled *The Devil's Birthday*, one of the definitive histories of that particular campaign.

Once the companies of the battalion had been formed, the training programme commenced in earnest under the direction of Squadron Leader W. ('Big Bill') Brereton and Lieutenant Law. Training was undertaken at Willingdon Airfield near Delhi using Vickers Valencia aircraft. These were lumbering vintage-style twin-engined biplanes, made in 1925, and the pilot and observer sat in an open cockpit at the front. The paratroopers were required to exit the aircraft through a bath-shaped hole knocked in the bottom of the aircraft. If the exiting manoeuvre was not carried out precisely the unfortunate paratrooper would hit his head on the hatch, generally resulting in a bloody or a broken nose. This painful event was known as 'ringing the bell.'

The tough training programme consisted of one week's solid PT under RSM McNary, followed by parachute training in the second week consisting of five jumps from the Valencia aircraft. Half the course undertook their jumps in the morning; the parachutes were then re-packed and used again by the other half of the course, who jumped in the afternoon. However the programme was bedevilled by setbacks, often caused by lack of equipment. At one point only three Valencia aircraft were available and only twenty parachutes had been brought out from England. Parachute training had just commenced with these meagre resources when all three aircraft were removed to assist in the evacuation of civilians from Burma following the Japanese invasion of that country. When the aircraft were eventually returned, parachute training was still held up because further supplies of parachutes sent from England had been lost due to enemy action, as well as some on their way to India via Egypt which were 'diverted' by Colonel David Stirling to his newly-formed special forces unit.

Shortages in equipment and supplies for the battalion even extended to such basic items (if that is the right description) as toilet paper. Bernard told me of George once recounting the story about the battalion being paraded one morning so that he could issue particular instructions on the use and conservation of these limited, and vitally important, stocks until further supplies were received.

The delays to parachute training caused by lack of equipment could easily have an effect on the morale of a unit particularly, as in this case, when it is has been formed from volunteers in the confident expectation of being quickly sent into action against the enemy. This dip in morale could then lead, in turn, to disciplinary problems, or, in George's more diplomatic words, for these hand-picked soldiers to become 'slightly browned off'. Christmas 1941, for example, was celebrated rather too well by some soldiers and resulted in damage to various bars/restaurants in Delhi. During the subsequent court martial of a sergeant, a witness was asked 'and where was the RSM at the time?' The answer - 'he was in the sergeants' mess, sitting astride a barrel of beer'

The courts martial records held at the National Archives show that two sergeants from 151 Parachute Battalion were tried by court martial at about that time in January 1942. The records indicate that both sergeants were charged with acting to the prejudice of good order and military discipline. One was found guilty and reduced to the ranks, while the other was found not guilty. Lt Col Lindsay then made the whole battalion do a punishment march of 30 miles during New Year's night, which the men are reported to have taken 'in remarkably good cheer', apparently because some of the water bottles had been illicitly filled with something very much stronger.

One training exercise in February 1942 involved the entire battalion and required that they be dropped to 'capture' the bridges over the Hindon River on the road between Delhi and Meerut. Only one aircraft was available to carry the battalion headquarters, so it was decided that the rest of the battalion should be 'dropped' from Indian buses. This might have seemed like a good idea at the time, but having troops jump out of moving buses is probably more dangerous than jumping out of an aeroplane. Of the ten men in one stick, one man was killed and the battalion's Intelligence Officer suffered severe concussion.

In addition to numerous training exercises, the battalion was required to carry out various other duties, such as participation in a ceremonial march-past in Delhi honouring the Chinese Marshall Chiang Kai-shek. Marching with the battalion in this large and important parade must have brought back strong memories for George of similar ceremonies carried out during his earlier service in the Coldstream Guards.

A particularly memorable, and more positive, event of the training programme took place in April, when the battalion undertook a gruelling 50-mile route march in 22 hours. The training programme required that the entire brigade - British, Indian and Gurkha battalions - were to march 60 miles in 24 hours in competition with each other. The battalions had to converge on Dehra Dun along three separate routes, and the Gurkha battalion were the firm favourites to win. The men of 151 Battalion were firstly taken by lorry from their cantonments in Delhi to an assembly area 60 miles from Dehra Dun, and at 1930 hours on the 19th April 1942, set out on the march to that city. It was a 'regulated route march', meaning that the troops were in fighting order, wearing shirts and shorts. Although there was a ten-minute halt every half hour, the battalion continued marching through the night. There was a halt at 0130 hrs which enabled the troops to change socks and get some sleep, but the battalion was on the move again at 0300 hrs.

George's typewritten history of the battalion, written in about 1944/45 when he was in the Glider Pilot Regiment, records that they had to then 'set about the hard task of climbing the 'khuds' by way of the Timli Pass, over 3,000 feet high and a tortuous, rocky road which seemed to have more twists and turns in it than a corkscrew'. Arriving at Timli village at about noon, the troops had a break which provided the opportunity to wash, shave, change socks and cook a meal in the mess tins. George wrote that 'All of our food for this march was Composite Rations, 'hard tack' plus nuts and raisins, which most of us preferred'. There was still another 22 miles to complete before arrival at Dehra Dun, and the battalion set off again at 1330 hrs and, again according to George, 'plodded along a first class tarmac road'.

The battalion was only 10 miles from the Dehra Dun finishing point when the Brigadier intercepted the column to say that the Indian and Gurkha battalions had fallen out and the British were therefore worthy winners. The battalion was then transported by lorry to Dehra Dun. This victory had been achieved, in George's words, 'under a pitiless Indian sun' and at a pace which left feet feeling like 'lumps of liver'. A 1950 edition of *Pegasus* magazine recalled this and other route marches with a heartfelt comment that 'not a few regretted that Colonel Martin Lindsay had walked twice across Greenland'.

Apart from shortages in parachuting and other equipment, the battalion suffered from its location being virtually on the doorstep of GHQ India, which consisted of old-fashioned senior British officers of the Indian Army. Martin Lindsay was recently described by Colonel John Waddy as an 'energetic, innovative and go-ahead parachute soldier' whose skills in creating this new formation were entirely unappreciated by these GHQ armchair soldiers. They were also simply unable to understand the concept of airborne forces, so they schemed and plotted for the battalion to be broken up. However it received the full support of Field Marshall Sir Archibald Wavell, the British Commander-in-Chief in India, who said 'There's nothing wrong with that battalion. All they need is to get into a proper battle'. Nonetheless a large scale Court of Inquiry was still held into the state of the battalion, which it then passed with flying colours.

Lt Colonel Lindsay left the Battalion in May and returned to England, being later replaced by Lt Colonel M C R Hose from the Beds & Herts Regiment. Lt Colonel Hose had been awarded the DSO (Distinguished Service Order) during the fighting at Tobruk, but he was not in the same mould as his predecessor. Martin Lindsay was very much admired and respected by the men under his command, and John Waddy recalled that 'it was a sad day when he left'.

By June 1942 the battalion was fully trained in all arms and fit for action, but still only about one third of the soldiers were qualified parachutists. During that month, under the temporary command of Major 'Mickey' Thomas, the battalion undertook combined operations training at Lake Karanwasla, approximately 12 miles from Poona. Major Thomas was later to return to his original regiment; he was killed in action during the D Day invasion of Normandy in 1944. The battalion's training included the use of invasion landing craft of various types, and was carried out under the guidance of petty officers of the Royal Indian Navy. Some officers nevertheless regarded this training as rather farcical, because many of the boats available were simply old lifeboats with manual oars.

The real reason behind this particular exercise may well have been simply to get the battalion away from Delhi for a while on its own and rebuild morale after the earlier unfounded criticisms by GHQ staff. The weather for the start of these activities was ideal but, during the following week, the monsoon broke. The rain fell night and day for the next three weeks and it seemed as if the battalion's tents would be washed into the lake. Despite this awful weather, the morale of the battalion did indeed improve, and all troops enjoyed the training on the hilly country around the lake, which came as a welcome change to Delhi's oppressive heat.

The battalion returned to Delhi in July and continued its parachute training, which was followed in August by deployment on internal security duties. There was also a successful action when troops taken from all three battalions and under the command of Lt Lee and Sgt Dixon of 151 battalion were parachuted into the Punjab area to intercept parties of Hurs terrorists. By September parachute training was being speeded up, with better Wellington aircraft being used, but this rushed training resulted in an increase in fatalities. One young officer, for example, started his course only a few days after arriving in the battalion, did his first jump on his first day of the course and was killed when his parachute malfunctioned.

On the 20th October 1942 George's acting rank of RSM was made substantive and, at the same time, 151 Battalion was formally mobilised. It was inspected by Field Marshall Sir Archibald Wavell on the following day, and subsequently renumbered 156 Battalion for security reasons before embarking for the Middle East at the end of the month. George meanwhile had been transferred out of the battalion pending his return to England in December.

John Waddy wrote to me saying '151 (British) Parachute Bn formed so long ago in Delhi had a short violent end a long way away in Holland 3 years later' The route to that violent end began after the battalion's arrival in Egypt on the 20th November 1942 where it was subsequently to form the nucleus for the newly created 4th Parachute Brigade. In March 1943 the brigade was moved to Palestine, with 156 Battalion being based at Jenin, where it was placed under the command of Lieut Colonel Sir Richard des Voeux.

The battalion next took part in the September 1943 invasion of Italy, being landed at the port of Taranto from the US Navy Cruiser *Bose* rather than dropped by aeroplane. After acquitting itself magnificently in the fighting against both Italian and German forces, the battalion was transferred to England in December, where it was initially stationed in the Uppingham area of Rutland before being concentrated round the market town of Melton Mowbray in Leicestershire. There then followed a series of abandoned operations during the summer of 1944 before the battalion formed part of the 1st Airborne Division's attempt to capture the bridge over the River Rhine at Arnhem in September 1944. This was part of the famous operation known as 'Market Garden'.

156 Parachute Battalion were flown across the North Sea

to drop into Holland during the afternoon of Market Garden's second day (18th September) when heavy and sustained fighting was already well under way. John Waddy's description of subsequent events, which he has kindly allowed me to quote, tells the battalion's story far better than I could:

Flying through thickening flak the battalion lost one aircraft shot down with the loss of 19 men and a further 12 men from enemy fire on the Drop Zone. On that night advancing towards Arnhem the leading company met heavy opposition at Oosterbeek station, and during the next morning in a series of fierce company actions to seize the Lichtenbeek feature, the battalion was badly cut up in the Johanna Hoeve Woods against heavy opposition by German panzer troops. In the subsequent withdrawal the battalion became split by the railway near Wolfheze but the main part pushed on during the next day through the woods towards Oosterbeek.

Increasing enemy pressure from all sides took a further heavy toll, including the loss of the Commanding Officer and the second-in-command, until eventually a small handful of men, led by Brigadier Shan Hackett, charged through into the perimeter which was taking shape. The battalion, numbering no more than 50 men under Major Geoffrey Powell, fought on in the houses and gardens in the vital northern sector of the narrow perimeter for a further 5 days until finally on orders of Field Marshall Montgomery, the remnants of the division were withdrawn over the river Rhine on the rainy night of 25th-26th September. The last few of the 156 Battalion, 28 in all, marched back to Driel, sadly depleted but not defeated, and then via Nijmegen flew back to their home base at Melton Mowbray.

By the time that they were gathered back in England, the battalion's total survivors numbered only about 120 men, from a starting figure of some 650. After a few weeks at Melton, they were sent on to Grimsthorpe in Lincolnshire, to be amalgamated with a similar number of men from the 1st Parachute Battalion. Thus 151/156 Parachute Battalion ceased to exist and so disappeared from the rolls. However the Battalion's unflagging spirit continues in its present thriving Old Comrades Association, of which I am very proud to be an Associate Member.

On the 17th December 1942, on his return to England, George was posted to the Parachute Regiment Depot, where he was employed on training and administrative duties connected with the establishment of the new depot. This was located at Hardwick Hall near Chesterfield in Derbyshire, and had been formed that same year in the grounds of the 16th Century Elizabethan mansion built by Elizabeth Countess of Shrewsbury (Bess of Hardwick). The site of the depot has since been completely cleared, and the only reminder of its existence is a memorial in the car park to the north of the mansion. The War Establishment for the depot was approved by the War Office on the 25th December 1942, and Lt Colonel W. Giles (Ox and Bucks Light Infantry) was its first Commanding Officer. The depot consisted of a depot company, a pre-parachute training company, a battle school, holding company and an airfield detachment which was stationed at No 1 Parachute Training School (PTS), RAF Ringway.

By the time of George's arrival in England, Evelyn, Bernard and Marion had already returned to live in Nottingham, staying with various friends and family members there. One such was Evelyn's sister Gladys and brother-in-law Alex Measures, with whom Evelyn had stayed when Bernard was born. They had moved on from their earlier home and now lived at 27 Fulwood Crescent on the Apsley Estate.

At the beginning of 1943 the 10th (T.A.) Battalion of The Essex Regiment was converted to an airborne unit, being renamed 9th Battalion (Eastern and Home Counties) Parachute Regiment, Army Air Corps. It was then despatched from its Essex base to Kiwi Barracks in Bulford Wiltshire as part of the newly formed 6th Airborne Division. The first soldiers from the battalion to undergo parachute training at Ringway were 14 Officers and 158 Other Ranks who attended course No 47 lasting from the 18th January to the 1st February. Pre-training exercises will have been carried out at the Parachute Regiment's Depot where George will have had his first contact with this particular unit.

The 10th Battalion's C.O. (Lt Col T E Hearn) had been too old to jump, so he had been replaced in February by Lt Col S J L Hill DSO MC, who therefore became the first Commanding Officer of the 9th Battalion. However Lt Col Hill's tenure of command was short lived, because he was soon promoted to the command of 3rd Parachute Brigade, which included the 9thBattalion. Lt Col Martin Lindsay then took command on the 2nd June and immediately sent for George to join him. George's orders did not require him to take up his new post until the 30th June, but Martin Lindsay was anxious to continue the battalion's conversion to a first-class parachute unit, and so wanted George working with him as soon as possible. It was therefore just over two weeks early, on the 14th June 1943, that he reported to take up duties as RSM, replacing the battalion's existing Acting RSM.

With such a rapid turnover in commanding officers, and with numerous changes in personnel, the battalion was going through a period of upheaval which might not have been welcomed by everyone. Certainly the war diary note of George's arrival carries a distinct whiff of disapproval as the original RSM is transferred elsewhere: Getting his first initial wrong, the entry records that 'RSM R E Gaunt reported to take up duties with the Bn… A/RSM W G Newland who had held the post since 6th Nov 1942 and had been with the Bn since its earliest days was posted to No 3 Inf Depot Southend'. Perhaps the writer of the diary thought the Acting RSM should have been made permanent? Nonetheless, George was soon to show his worth to the battalion.

George had clearly developed a very good working relationship with Martin Lindsay, who had sought his transfer to 9th Battalion. The background to this request was explained to me in a 1995 letter from Terrence Otway, who was later to assume command of the battalion. Colonel Otway wrote that 'As a CO of a newly formed unit one usually made certain that one had as one's RSM someone one knew and trusted.' Major General Julian Thompson later wrote of the RSM as being 'the commanding officer's right-hand man and advisor on many aspects of the battalion/regiment daily life, especially matters involving the soldiers and NCOs. The CO and the RSM have very likely known each other since the former was a second lieutenant and the latter was a young private or equivalent'. George had only known Lt Colonel Lindsay for two years, so it is indicative of the high regard in which he was held that Lt Colonel Lindsay should specifically ask for George to be his RSM.

Just as he had in India, Lt Col Lindsay quickly established himself as 'an unorthodox and imaginative leader'. This was a description applied to him by Napier Crookenden, who was appointed to command the battalion in mid June 1944. Napier Crookenden's book *Dropzone Normandy* describes how Lt Col Lindsay once ordered that any man who had completed 15 parachute jumps could wear parachute wings on both shoulders instead of solely on the right shoulder as provided by Army regulations.

I think this was a good example of Lt Colonel Lindsay's somewhat individualistic approach to the treatment of British Army uniforms. He appears to have considered, for example, that new units under his command should not be constrained by the usual approach to the display of unit badges such as applied elsewhere in the Army. The issuing of the order was, almost inevitably, followed by the prompt appearance of a parachute jump balloon in the barrack square with a line of soldiers from the 9th Battalion queuing to go up and parachuting back down, thereby 'qualifying' for their extra wings. This order was very shortly afterwards directly cancelled by Brigadier Hill; an indication, perhaps, that these two officers may not have always seen eye-to-eye with each other.

On another occasion Lt Colonel Lindsay took exception to the continued use of a particular four-letter swear word used by the men under his command. Accordingly he ordered that any man heard using the word should be placed under close arrest. However this resulted in such a rapid filling of the cells in the Guardroom that the order was quickly and quietly forgotten.

Taking regular drill parades formed an important part of George's duties as RSM, and the battalion's Training Instructions referred to their importance. Instruction No 2 stated: 'RSM's Parades will be held at frequent intervals to improve the general standard of smartness and bearing'. The training programme for Wednesday 4th August shows the RSM taking Drill Parades at 0830, 1145 and 1500, with the presentation of a lecture on the 'Duties of NCOs' at 1100. The programme for September 1943 shows the RSM's Drill Parade at 0830 on Monday 13th of that month.

George was stationed at Bulford when he met Kathleen Wiltshire, who was the manageress of Osmond's Café and a number of other businesses located in the Bulford Camp Market. This was situated just off Bond Street in an area known as 'tin town', because so many of the buildings were constructed of corrugated iron. The market was swept away during the Camp's redevelopment during the late 1960s, and the site is now a car park. Although both George and Kathleen were married with children (Kathleen had a three-year-old daughter, Valerie), they had both grown apart from their respective spouses. Kathleen's husband William was stationed nearby with the Royal Artillery, while Evelyn was still living near Nottingham with Bernard and Marion.

Kathleen was at that time living with her parents Arthur and Rose Williams. Arthur worked as a storeman for the Army, and they all lived in a house by the name of Carna in Ratfyn Road, Amesbury, only a couple of miles from Bulford. Also living in the house was Kathleen's sister Marjorie, who taught at the local school, and her one-year old daughter, Myfanwy. The house was a three-bedroom semi-detached property so with four adults and two children it must have been very full indeed. Marjorie's husband, Richard Jones, was also serving with the Royal Artillery.

Kathleen's account of their meeting, told to me shortly before she died, recalled the day she was working in the café while two young paratroopers were present, having nipped in for a quick tea break. They were just leaving the premises and returning to duty when they spotted George's stern figure coming down the road. Despite ducking hurriedly back into the café, it was obvious that they had been seen, and that the RSM was now heading in their direction. Explaining their situation to Kathleen, the worried paratroopers told her that they weren't supposed to be there and would be in serious trouble if they were caught. The RSM was now heading for the front door. Kathleen quickly ushered the two soldiers into the back of the building and helped them escape by letting them sneak out through the rear exit. Quickly rushing back into the seating area, Kathleen removed the tell-tale teacups and was polishing the table when the door was flung open and the RSM swept into the café.

'Where are they?' he demanded, eyes scanning the room, swagger stick under his arm.

'Where are who?' Kathleen innocently responded, straightening up from her polishing, cleaning cloth in hand.

'The two men I saw about to leave the café. They know they're not permitted here at this time of day.'

'I'm very sorry' Kathleen replied, calmly looking around the room 'But I haven't a clue what you're talking about. There aren't any soldiers in here - as you can very well see.'

I think George must have been absolutely astonished by this response. He knew what he'd witnessed and, although he had not been able to recognise the men, he also knew that finding out who they were and imposing his discipline was a simple, straightforward task. Here he was, an important and respected member of the battalion, a man used to being obeyed and whose word was law. He was the confidant of the CO, and was consulted by the Adjutant; officers addressed him as 'Mister'. Hard-bitten NCOs got edgy when he was around and recruits trembled in his presence. Yet this café manageress was now challenging him by flatly denying the very existence of the two soldiers he had seen, who had apparently just disappeared into thin air!

Wholly unaccustomed to this type of reaction, and unable to overcome her defiance, George was left with no option but to leave the café and go on his way.

Nevertheless Kathleen had obviously struck a spark with George. This may have been due to the fact that she had stood up to him, and not been overawed by his obvious sense of authority. Possibly he had also seen in her a strength of character which appealed to him and which had been so obviously demonstrated by his mother during his formative years. He therefore asked Kathleen to go out with him on various occasions afterwards, although in later years she used to say that she tried to discourage him.

Then one day, a friend of hers, Dorothy Daykin, invited her to go to an afternoon tea dance in Salisbury. Little did Kathleen know that George and Dorothy had secretly conspired to arrange the invitation. Having boarded the bus, the two friends were chatting happily when it pulled up at the next stop and, much to Kathleen's surprise, George got on wearing his best suit and going to the same dance. Kathleen found herself with no option but to allow George to accompany her, and their relationship developed from then onwards.

It must have been at some point after this time that George took Kathleen to Beeston to meet his sister Flo and her husband Walter Ross, who were living in Montague Street. This led to the incident which resulted in Bernard discovering the bombshell that his parents had parted. At that time Evelyn, Bernard and Marion were living in Derby Street, about half a mile away, and somehow Evelyn had learnt about George and Kathleen's visit. She then summoned Bernard and sent him on an errand to his Auntie Flo, telling him that he could see his dad there. Rushing excitedly over to Montague Street, Bernard was horrified and very upset to find his Dad in the company of a woman other than his mother.

After George began his relationship with Kathleen, he had very little to do with his original family except to make maintenance payments, although a post-war Army document does list his 'next-of-kin (other than wife)' as his son, 'Bernard Ronald Gaunt'. I do think this is an enlightening choice, because if George had completely severed all links with his previous family, he could easily have listed one of his siblings, Lyn or Flo. His choice of Bernard seems to me to indicate that he must have still felt some connection with his son. Bernard however was wholly unaware of this and was very much adversely affected by George's actions. He felt that his father had willingly abandoned him, which left him feeling utterly rejected and also, I am quite sure, betrayed, so it was to be very many years later before he was able to forgive his father for this act.

Marion adored George hugely and also felt his departure very deeply indeed. Evelyn, not unnaturally, was also very bitter towards George, keeping Bernard in the dark about all George's maintenance payments to her and portraying George as the villain of the piece in the breakdown of the marriage. She eventually remarried in 1947.

During this time the training programme for the 9th Parachute Battalion continued in accordance with the Training Directive issued by the Divisional Commander, Major-General Richard Gale OBE MC. This directive contained the tasks for which the 6th Airborne Division was to prepare, all designed to help a seaborne invasion. They included an attack on a coastal battery, the seizing of ground vital to the advance of the main assault forces and the blocking of enemy reserves approaching the bridgehead area. The training programme paid special attention to physical fitness and endurance, because every ounce of equipment and ammunition required by the battalion had to be carried by the men. They would also be facing numerically superior and more heavily-armed opponents. Parachute jumping by day and night was also practised, and much time and effort was put into the problem of rallying the men into a formed group after the drop.

In a note on the training of Parachute Troops in 1943,

Brigadier Hill laid considerable emphasis on both discipline and physical fitness, and regular route marches contributed to the fitness regime. One such route march occurred in August 1943, when the battalion marched from Bulford to Bath as a 'warm up' before a major exercise. The exercise ended after eight days, and the battalion found itself at Blandford in Dorset, very hot and tired but much relieved to see transport waiting to return the men to Bulford. To the dismay of the soldiers however, Lt Colonel Lindsay then dismissed the transport and ordered the battalion to march the 30 miles or so back to the barracks.

The training programme was relentless. Shortly afterwards the battalion was sent on a training exercise in the Highlands of Scotland, where the battalion's diary records that the 'RSM will be Officer i/c Transport'. Parachute drops were carried out in the area of Boat of Garten and in the Spey valley. The training was also mixed with a recruiting drive although records do not show the success or otherwise of that particular activity.

Returning overnight from Edinburgh to London on the 18-19th August, the battalion was met on its arrival at Kings Cross Station by the band of the Essex Regiment. There followed a parade through London along Shaftesbury Avenue, Charing Cross Road, The Strand, Fleet Street and Moorgate to a Drill Hall in Sun Street, where the salute was taken by Major-General Gale. An unusual feature of the battalion's uniform on the parade is that the soldiers continued to wear the cap badge of the Essex Regiment rather than the Airborne Forces cap badge, which had yet to be issued. After a lunch for members of the battalion and their families, the men dispersed for nine days' privilege leave.

However, not all training was outdoors. One 'cloth model' exercise under the direction of Majors Otway and Parry took place on the 26th November in the Billiard Room of the Officers Mess at Bulford, where company officers and NCOs (including RSM Gaunt) were divided into five syndicates. A 'Cloth Model Exercise' is an indoor training exercise allowing commanders to plan or rehearse a battle sequence using a cloth covered table-top model of the location or the type of terrain in which the fighting is to take place. The exercise can also be carried out by using a sand table model, though it is nowadays more commonly undertaken with the use of computers. The object of the exercise in this particular case was 'To study the lessons learnt during the past two months' relating to the 'correct procedure for a parachute company during the four phases' of a paratroop operation.

George left the 9th Parachute Battalion on the 31st December 1943, having been posted to the nearby Glider Pilot Depot. Terence Otway, who was the battalion's second-in-command at the time, recalled the news of George's posting, writing that 'much to his disgust and my disappointment your father was told that because of his injury and his age he would have to leave the battalion.' Colonel Otway further described George's departure as 'a great blow' because he believed George to be 'largely responsible for the fact that we considered the 9th to be the best battalion in 6th Airborne Division.' The reference to George's age highlights the fact that he had just turned 40, which was really very old for a front-line paratrooper, particularly when compared to the average age of a mere 20 years for the soldiers under his charge. After all, as the old saying has it, 'war is a young man's game.'

The mention of George's injury must have referred to an injury of 'moderate severity' which he had sustained on the 22nd September. His Army medical records are woefully lacking in particulars, but I believe that the injury affected his leg. It may have also inflamed an earlier injury, apparently 'of a trivial nature', which had occurred on 19th May, although his medical records are equally short of detail in that particular case. Kathleen always maintained that the latest injury happened during training, but one story I heard contends that it actually came about during a hard-fought football match between members of the 9th Battalion and 1st Canadian Parachute Battalion, which also formed part of the 3rd Parachute Brigade.

These Canadian paratroopers had a less than entirely respectful approach to traditional British Army authority so often personified by the Regimental Sergeant Major, and George's involvement in the match appears to have been too much of a temptation for them. As George had the ball, he was apparently energetically tackled by a number of Canadians who seem to have taken only a passing interest in kicking the actual football. As the resultant melee broke up George was on the ground, probably with a torn ligament or something similar. If this particular story is true, the irony of serving in a unit where injuries to the leg were almost commonplace during training, yet receiving it while engaged in a sporting activity must have hurt almost as much as the injury itself.

Whatever the cause of that injury, George was hospitalised for a while, probably at the Military Hospital in Tidworth, where Kathleen visited him as often as possible. He was then called before a Medical Board at Bulford on the 18th December, which re-graded his Medical Category from A1 to B2. The Medical Category 'A' essentially means fit for general service at home and abroad, while Category 'B' means fit for base or garrison service at home and abroad but not fit for general service abroad. The sub categories A1, A2, B1, B2 etc were based on such additional matters as vision in relation to shooting and driving, physical endurance and the ability to march. This regrading must have finally ended any lingering hopes that George might have harboured of taking a more active role in fighting for his country during the Second World War.

George's departure from the battalion was followed within a matter of months by that of Lt Colonel Lindsay. Having played a key role in the establishment of Airborne Forces, Lt Colonel Lindsay left in April 1944. His leaving was both unexpected and abrupt, although the reason is not apparently recorded. The battalion's War Diary for that day simply registers the change of command in one brief sentence: 'Major TBH Otway assumes comd of the Bn vice Lt Col M A Lindsay - relinquished'. Lindsay subsequently went to Normandy in late June, joining the 1st Battalion Gordon Highlanders. He was second in command, and at times in command, of that battalion until the end of the war. His book *So Few Got Through*, first published in 1946, is widely regarded as a descriptive masterpiece of life in an infantry battalion in North West Europe during 1944/45. He was awarded the DSO in April 1945 and later became Conservative MP for Solihull, being made a CBE in 1952. Sir Martin Lindsay Bt CBE DSO MP died in 1981.

Major Terence Otway had joined the battalion in July 1943, having previously served with 1st Battalion The Royal Ulster Rifles, a glider-borne unit of 6th Airborne Division. He was at home on leave when he received a telephone call from the Brigade Major telling him to report back to Bulford for an urgent meeting with Brigadier Hill. Even when he arrived at the Headquarters building on the 2nd April, Major Otway still had no idea as to why he had been so suddenly recalled from leave. He was quickly ushered into the office of Brigadier Hill to receive the somewhat startling news that he was now in command of the battalion.

Lt Colonel Otway and 9th Parachute Battalion went on to successfully undertake the difficult and daring assault on the Merville Gun Battery as part of 'Operation Tonga' during the night of the 5th - 6th June 1944 in advance of the D Day sea-borne landings. The battalion's assignment was described by Brigadier Hill in advance of the operation as a 'Grade A stinker of a job' and, much later, by American historian Stephen E. Ambrose in his book about D Day, as a 'brilliant feat of arms'. Having achieved their objective at Merville, the battalion went on to participate in the desperate fighting at Amfréville-Le-Plein, the Château St Come and the crossroads at le Mesnil as they fought to help protect the left flank of the Normandy invasion beachhead.

George was deeply upset to learn subsequently that his friend and replacement as RSM in 9 Parachute Battalion, William (Bill) Cunningham, had been killed in action on the 17th June. RSM Cunningham, who was recommended for the VC by Lt Colonel Otway for his courage under fire on 12th

June, is buried in Ranville Military Cemetery in Normandy (Grave IIA B12). Lt Colonel Otway was awarded the DSO in October 1944 in recognition of his conspicuous bravery and outstanding leadership during the actions at Merville and Le Mesnil. He died, at the age of 92, in July 2006.

The response to Churchill's call for 5,000 parachute troops in June 1940 was later to receive considerable impetus in May 1941, when the Germans made extensive use of paratroop and glider-borne soldiers in their successful invasion of the Mediterranean island of Crete. However at that time the RAF did not consider that they would be able to provide all the troop-carrying aircraft needed to carry the number of soldiers now being transferred to Britain's airborne forces, so the Army began to look at alternatives. There had been various early experiments in the use of military gliders, but the Army then saw how successful the Germans had apparently been in their use of gliders during the battle for Crete. It was therefore decided that a glider-borne force should also be created alongside the paratroops, and thus the Glider Pilot Regiment was born, officially established by an order of the 21st December 1941.

Despite initial RAF opposition, the decision was also made that the glider pilots should come under the command of the Army rather than the RAF. Brigadier George Chatterton, the Commander of the Glider Pilot Regiment, had insisted on the creation of a glider pilot force consisting of what he termed 'total soldiers'. Not only were they trained to pilot their craft safely and land them with pin-point accuracy, they could then be called upon to join in the subsequent action, fighting alongside their former passengers. Brigadier Chatterton summed it up when he wrote that 'in the Glider Pilot we would be trying to create a very special character - a highly-trained soldier as well as a skilful and resourceful pilot.'

Recruits for the Glider Pilot Regiment were sent to the Regiment's Depot at Fargo Camp near Larkhill on Salisbury Plain for a four-week initial training period. The regiment had moved to Fargo in September 1943 from their original 'Airborne Camp' at Tilshead, and remained there until the camp closed in 1946. George's role in this training of 'total soldiers' was to follow in the pattern established on the regiment's formation, when drill instructors had initially been recruited from the Brigade of Guards; the first two being CSM Michael Briody of the Irish Guards and CSM Jim Cowley of the Coldstream Guards. Brigadier Chatterton had wanted 'the very best NCOs as instructors', and George was particularly well qualified in that respect.

In a letter of March 1992 published in the magazine of the Glider Pilot Regiment Association, J Cadden recalled being 'thrown on the tender mercies of RSM Gaunt who taught us how to wear boots and 'stand up straight' again!' Another of those 'thrown on the tender mercies of RSM Gaunt' was Mr W. E. Hands, who had been posted to Fargo Camp at the end of February 1944, having previously served in the Royal Corps of Signals. He recalled how George 'gave us volunteers a hard time, but he was a very fair man'. Mr Hands' letter to me tells the tale of the 'Stick Man' (the neatest soldier on parade) being selected from those soldiers about to go on Guard Duty.

It is easy to picture the scene described by Mr Hands. A

detachment of soldiers is formed up and being inspected by the Duty Officer and, perhaps much more frighteningly, the Regimental Sergeant Major. The RSM has slowly walked in front and behind each rank of soldiers checking such items as the shine on boots and buckles, the sharpness of uniform creases, the straightness of belts and badges and the cleanliness of rifles. He then suddenly stops behind one very worried soldier, who is left wondering just what the RSM has found wrong. Leaning close to the soldier's ear, the RSM announces in a stage whisper 'You are the Stick Man for tonight.' The selected soldier was hugely relieved and very surprised by this act, which is why, 51 years later, Mr Hands was able to write 'so I remember your dad to this day'.

Mr. F. Bradley of the Regiment's 'A' Squadron wrote a letter relating his arrival at Fargo Camp 'on a hot summer afternoon in 1944'. He had previously served in a 'rather easy-going non-combatant unit' but then found himself being 'initiated in drill movements only normally seen I think on Horse Guards Parade and the like'. Commenting that 'the only contact with RSM Gaunt was on the parade ground', Mr Bradley went on to say 'throughout the weeks I was there RSM Gaunt's was a figure that commanded respect, a quiet authority I would say, with no stridency that I remember. Along with Michael Briody from the Irish Guards (he was a pilot) they were the two most notable WO1s of my army career, both I say without hesitation, gentlemen'.

Jack Porter was an RAF Sergeant Pilot who wrote to say that he was 'seconded to the GPR following the loss of so many glider pilots at Arnhem.' He was based at Fargo Camp between the 23rd February and the 23rd March 1945, and wrote that 'owing to the nature of our new jobs, it was of course necessary for the Army to try and make soldiers of us in the shortest possible time. This task was given to men like RSM Gaunt and a number of very high calibre NCOs from various regiments.' Jack recalled that his 'most vivid recollection' of George 'was this tall guardsman giving an immaculate display of rifle drill before our disbelieving gaze'. Jack went on to write that George 'was very popular with the men and had their universal respect. I reckon they would have followed him anywhere.' Jack concluded his letter by writing 'I know that distance lends enchantment and all that, but looking back at my experiences at Fargo and despite my ambition of becoming a fighter pilot being shattered, I reckon I almost enjoyed my stay there!'

Harry Ridgeway wrote to me from his home in the USA saying: "I joined the Glider Pilot Regiment at Fargo Camp Larkhill on the 26th June 1945 at which time your father was the RSM. I was then eighteen years old and had been in the regular army for two years having enlisted as a Royal Artillery 'Boy' at the age of sixteen. I recall your father vividly. When on parade he was everything that one would expect an RSM to be. However when off the parade ground your father was a quietly spoken fatherly type of man for whom I had great respect. He contributed to bringing me from boyhood to manhood'. In his letter Harry also echoed the sentiments of Mr Bradley, writing that 'if I should be called upon to describe your father in a single word I would choose to use the word 'gentleman'.'

George's History of 151 British Battalion describes his move from the Coldstream Guards to Airborne Forces, but gives no clue as to the reasons for that move. The records of his interviews both with Martin Lindsay and later with Lt Colonel Rock have not survived, so there is no officially-documented clue as to his reasons either. It may simply have been that the move offered promotion from Company Sergeant Major to Regimental Sergeant Major, but I think it was much more fundamental than that. George had been a professional soldier for 26 years and, with the outbreak of war, probably expected to be called upon to put all his training and skills into practice on the field of battle. Instead, he found himself transferred to a 'rear area' training role which he must have found to be hugely frustrating.

His qualifications as an instructor and his capabilities as an administrator, together with his age at the outbreak of war, meant that the Coldstream Guards were unlikely to use him in any other role, so it was doubtful if he would ever be directly involved in any combat while in that regiment. The creation of Airborne Forces on the other hand - a new force seeking skilled soldiers - could well provide the opportunity for the action to which all his training had led. It must therefore have been something of a disappointment subsequently for him to see his training/administration role simply being continued in Airborne Forces. However it almost certainly resulted in his surviving the war, because the airborne units with which he served suffered the most appalling numbers of casualties.

George and Flo.
Undated
photograph,
probably taken at
a school party.

Undated family
photograph taken
outside the front door
of 270 Broad Lane,
Bramley. Alfred, Annie,
Flo, Lyn and George.

Undated posed photograph. Flo, Alfred, George, Annie and Lyn.

Undated photograph of George, possibly as an apprentice.

Guardsman G E Gaunt 2652062. 14th Company 1st Battalion
Coldstream Guards. Guards Depot Caterham, Surrey, 16th June 1925.

Corporal Butler's Squad, Coldstream Guards, Caterham, July 1925. George is on the back row 2nd from left.

1st Battalion Coldstream Guards, winners of the Prince of Wales Rugby Cup 1930.
George is on the front row, second from the left.

((c) National Army Museum)

Evelyn, Bernard and Flo. Probably photographed in Nottingham circa 1930/31.

Photo taken at the British Barracks, Atbara, Sudan, August 1932. George is on the right.

Guard leaving Kasr-el-Nil Barracks in Cairo to do guard duty at Bab-el-Habib. Egypt 1933. George is at the rear of the detachment.

Field Marshall His Royal Highness Arthur Duke of Connaught visiting Pirbright Barracks, 5th September 1939.
George is the Colour Sergeant in full Guard Order.

WO11 (Company Sergeant Major) G E Gaunt. Coldstream Guards, 1940.

WO1 (Regimental Sergeant Major) G E Gaunt. Parachute Regiment, 1941.

George is wearing the pith helmet with the 151 (British) Parachute Battalion Flash on the side. The officer to his right is Major Mickey Thomas, while the third officer appears to be an RAF Squadron Leader. The group are probably watching, or waiting for, an early evening parachute drop. India 1941/42.

151 (British) Parachute Battalion marching along Kingsway in Delhi to honour Marshall Chiang Kai-shek, May 1942. Major Gaitley is leading, followed by Captain Gilchrist, RSM Gaunt, Captain Satterthwaite and 'A' Company.

(Airborne Forces Museum)

Warrant Officers and Sergeants of 9th Parachute Battalion, Bulford 1943. The Battalion's Commanding Officer, Lt Colonel M A Lindsay, is seated at the front centre with RSM G E Gaunt on his right.

RSM GE Gaunt.
Glider Pilot Regiment Depot, Fargo Camp Larkhill, 1944.

Inspecting the Guard. Glider Pilot Regiment Depot, Fargo Camp 1944.

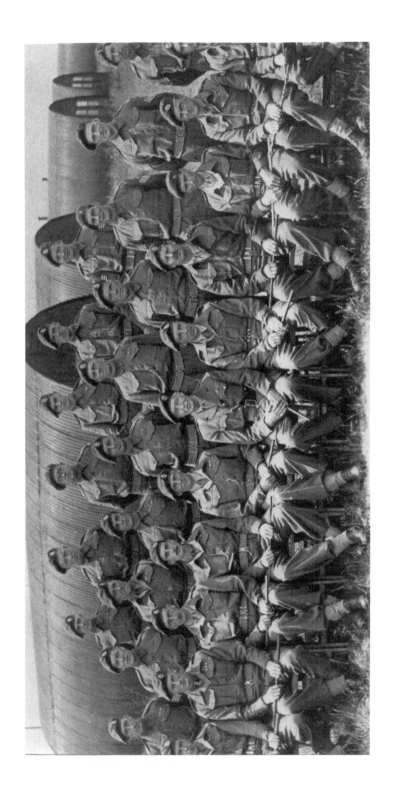

Glider Pilot Regiment, Fargo Camp June 1945. George is in the middle row, 5th from the right.

(Museum of Army Flying)

George and Kathleen. Wedding photograph, 22nd June 1946.

Lt (QM) George Gaunt. Royal Army Service Corps, 1946.

George in the garden of 'New Aloes' Europa Road Gibraltar,
16 October 1946.

Officers of 33 Company RASC, New Mole Barracks Gibraltar 1947.
George is in the centre of the back row.

New Year's Eve Ball 1947. George and Kathleen are in the middle of the
group. Alan and Hilary Miall are the only others in this group whose
names are known. They are on the left of the picture.

George and Kathleen photographed in
Trafalgar Square. 7 September 1948.

Dad holding me outside the
Officers' Mess, Bulford 1952.

A photograph from the Isle of Wight, 1951. Left to right - Kathleen,
Valerie, George (holding his nephew Andrew Ross), Walter Ross and
Peggy Ross (George's brother-in-law and niece).

The Eliot Arms, South Cerney. Circa 1953/54.

Mum, Dad, Flo and Walter Ross pictured behind the Saloon Bar counter, 1955. It is possible that this photograph was taken at the same time as the next two.

Dad pulling a pint while Mum smiles at the photographer, 1955.

Watched by Dad, Mum is presenting an inscribed tankard to
Mr G Savory, winner of an open darts tournament held at the Eliot.
The fact that Mr Savory is wearing his raincoat may indicate that the
presentation took place some time after the tournament - probably to
allow time for the tankard to be inscribed. March 1955.

This is me sitting on the empty beer barrels which are awaiting collection by the draymen. Behind is the corrugated iron coal shed/wood store, while to the right, behind the just-visible tricycle, is the gents' toilet. Note that the yard has not yet been surfaced in tarmac. Circa 1956.

Taking Valerie to
All Hallows Church,
South Cerney,
2nd September 1961.

Rothschild can write a few words on paper and make it worth £1,000,000—

That's Capital

A navvy can move tons of earth per day and earn seven shillings—

That's Labour

Some few tradesmen do not study their customers—

That's a Mistake

A man can run a business for a time and not advertise—

That's Foolishness

Solomon had six hundred wives and slept with his father—

That's Wisdom

George Gaunt will be pleased to see old and new customers, and have the pleasure of supplying them with the very best of Wines, Spirits and Beers—

That's Business

"Happy Days."

The
Eliot Arms
SOUTH CERNEY

FULLY LICENSED

■

Licensee :
G. E. GAUNT

■

BED AND BREAKFAST

■

Service a speciality

Hospitality certain

■

LOCAL FISHING

STANDARD PRINTING WORKS.

Advice and Poetry

Free to sit and free to think,
Free to pay for what you drink ;
Free to stop an hour or so,
When uneasy, free to go.

A Tanner in the Pocket is worth more than THREE on a Horse.

My beer is good, my measure just,
Forgive me please, I cannot trust ;
I've trusted many, to my sorrow,
So pay to-day and owe to-morrow.

My clock ticks but I don't.

Today I don't cash cheques, tomorrow I may.

2 Pints make	... ...	1 Quart
4 Quarts make	... ...	1 Gallon
1 Argument makes	...	1 Quarrel
1 Quarrel makes	...	1 Fight
1 Fight makes	...	2 Policeman
1 Magistrate ...	...	20/- or 14 days

When you swear, swear by your country,
When you steal, steal away from bad company.

When you drink, DRINK at

The Eliot Arms

CALL FREQUENTLY
DRINK MODERATELY
PAY HONOURABLY
BE GOOD COMPANY
PART FRIENDLY
GO HOME QUIETLY

I have been pleasing and displeasing the public ever since I started in business.

I have also been cussed and discussed, robbed, lied to, held up, hung up, and knocked up.

The only reason I am staying in business is to see what the hell will happen next.

Life is just one damned thing after another.

Business card produced by Dad, circa 1959

Wedding group at the church, 2nd September 1961. Left to right: Jock Plain, Andrew Plain, Charlie Clayton-Carter, Mollie Plain, Brian Painter, Colin, Valerie, Margaret Plain, Kathleen Gaunt, Alan Gaunt, Rose Williams, George Gaunt.

Wedding guests from Dad's side of the family. Left to right: Lyn Grimshaw, Elsie Grimshaw, Janet Grimshaw, Peter Roberts, Walter Ross, Flo Ross, Alan Gaunt, Don Grimshaw, Kathleen Gaunt, Peggy Roberts, George Gaunt, Andrew Ross. Outside South Cerney Village Hall, with the River Churn behind, 2nd September 1961.

The Eliot Arms, South Cerney. Photographed
on a rainy day in March 1964.

The Eliot Arms Public Bar. Left to right: Marjorie Jones, George Gaunt,
Elsie Grimshaw, Richard Jones, Cyril Cox, VI Binns, Kathleen Gaunt,
Viv Cox and, nearly out of shot, Wilf Curtis. March 1964.

The Eliot Arms' league-winning cribbage team. Standing left to right: Bill Huxley, Ron Lockey, Viv Cox, Tony Hunter, George Gaunt and Richard Jones. Seated: Kathleen Gaunt, Dick Selby (who presented the trophy) and Winnie Beard. Monday 25th May 1964.

Dad and Mum behind the counter in the saloon bar of the Eliot Arms, circa 1964. The curtains behind Dad give access to the public bar.

Dad and Mum outside the Eliot Arms' front porch. Note that Dad is wearing slippers because of his swollen feet. Circa 1964.

Mum and Dad attending the wedding of Don Grimshaw to Jean Farnell, 29 August 1964.

A photograph of the large sitting room at 8 Station Road, viewed from the hall. It shows the Victorian fireplace which covered the original inglenook.

A slightly grainy shot of Dad and me (with Punch) in the garden of 8 Station Road, circa 1964. The area in the foreground of the photo was cleared and replaced with a gravel surface to provide parking space for cars. The wall and single gate in the background were replaced by double metal gates.

The 16th Century gravestone in the wall of the barn at 8 Station Road. Photographed in 1967 after the Ivy covering the wall had been removed.

A photograph showing the front of 8 Station Road in 1999.

Dad and Mum (holding Simon Plain) with Rose Williams in the back garden of the Eliot, 1965. The tin building behind is 'the Hut' and the stone wall was the original rear boundary wall of the Eliot.

The Eliot Arms public bar, 1965. Left to right: Joe Bolton, George Allaway, Mr Daffin, Unknown, Kathleen Gaunt, Alan Gaunt, George Gaunt, Elsie Grimshaw, Unknown, Jim Price, Mr Caswell.

'The happy reunion'. Back row left to right: Alan Gaunt, Shirley Gaunt, Don Grimshaw, Bernard Gaunt, Jo Gaunt. Front row: Flo Ross, Stuart Gaunt, Jean Grimshaw, Jenny Gaunt. 19th March 1995.

The brothers -
Bernard and
Alan Gaunt.
18th March 1995.

The Eliot Arms, South Cerney 1953-1967

Plan 1 - Outbuildings and Land

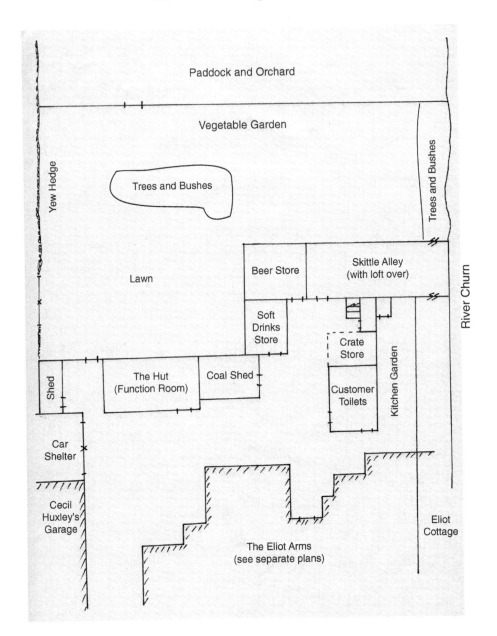

Paddock and Orchard

Vegetable Garden

Yew Hedge

Trees and Bushes

Trees and Bushes

River Churn

Lawn

Beer Store

Skittle Alley
(with loft over)

Soft
Drinks
Store

Crate
Store

Kitchen Garden

Shed

The Hut
(Function Room)

Coal Shed

Customer
Toilets

Car
Shelter

Cecil
Huxley's
Garage

Eliot
Cottage

The Eliot Arms
(see separate plans)

The Eliot Arms, South Cerney 1953-1967
Plan 2 - Ground Floor

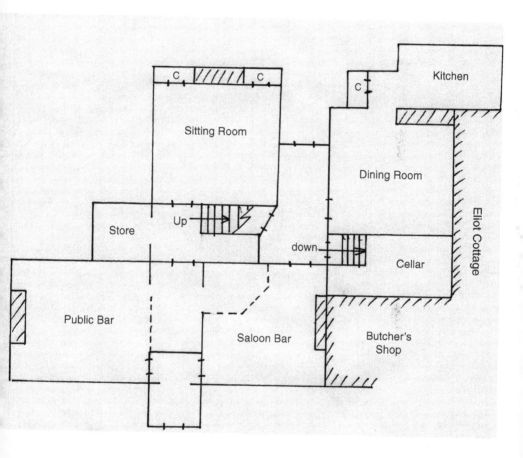

The Eliot Arms, South Cerney 1953-1967

Plan 3 - First Floor

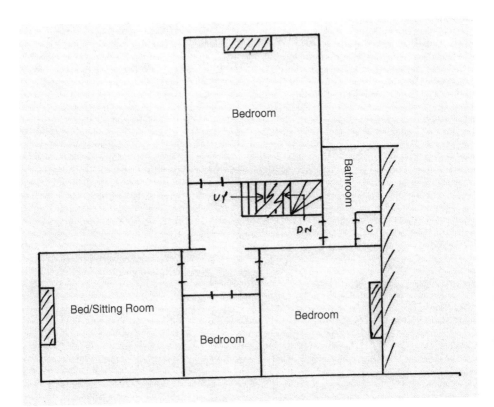

The Eliot Arms, South Cerney 1953-1967

Plan 4 - Second Floor

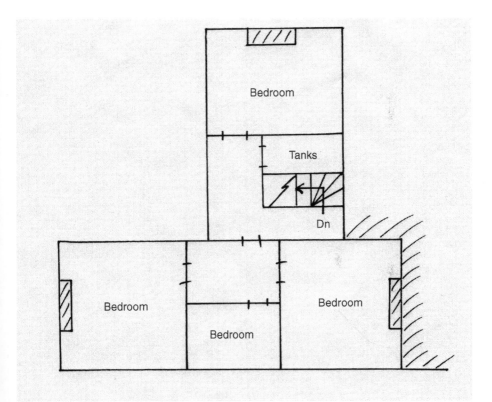

CHAPTER FIVE

THE POST-WAR PERIOD

And now – win the Peace! (1945 Election Slogan)

The final assessment of the non-commissioned period of George's Army service in 1945 records his military conduct as 'exemplary' and describes him as 'a thoroughly honest, sober and hardworking Warrant Officer.' The assessment goes on to state that 'In his long and varied military career he has risen to the top by carrying out the duties assigned to him in a very keen and efficient manner'. The assessment concludes that 'He has a fine record of service embellished by many qualifications.' The Certificate of Discharge describes George as being 5ft 11½' in height with grey eyes, fair hair and a fresh complexion. Although not stating his weight, the only difference between this description and that of twenty years earlier is that George is now apparently half an inch taller.

His Army documents show that on the 30th October 1945, shortly before his 42nd birthday, George was discharged from the Army Air Corps 'for the purposes of being appointed to a Commission' as a Lieutenant (Quarter Master) in the Royal Army Service Corps. This appointment came after a medical examination followed by an interview at Larkhill on the 4th August. The examination passed him fit for general service, although still in Medical Category B2, while the interview confirmed that he was 'likely to make an efficient Lieut (QM) RASC'. The appointment to a Commission was a remarkable achievement for George, because the Army is generally broken down very strictly into officers on the one hand and 'other ranks' on the other. To make the transition from other rank (even one as exalted as Regimental Sergeant Major) to officer is not an everyday occurrence and is generally limited to soldiers of the highest calibre.

The Army Service Corps dates from December 1888, when the Army's Commissariat and Transport Departments were amalgamated. The prefix 'Royal' was awarded to the Corps in 1918 as formal recognition of its courageous service during the First World War. The responsibilities of the Corps were widespread, and included such matters as land and coastal transport, air dispatch, the supply of food, water, fuel and general domestic stores such as clothing, furniture and stationery. It was also responsible for the administration of barracks, the Army Fire Service and the provision of staff clerks to Headquarters units. The RASC was replaced by the Royal Corps of Transport in 1965 which, in turn, later became part of the Royal Logistics Corps.

George's first posting was to Liverpool as Assistant Barrack Officer and then, on the 4th February 1946, he was posted to the Barrack Office in Chester, where he lived in the Militia Buildings. This was a very busy time for commissioned quartermasters such as George, who, according to the RASC history, 'constituted the real backbone of Barrack Services.' In this period following the end of the Second World War, and with the Army undergoing huge changes, barrack officers were heavily engaged in planning the conversion and re-equipping of barracks designated for peacetime use, which would replace the temporary wartime accommodation. This peacetime activity became doubly important as the popular press of the day began to focus on the levels of provision for the troops, and particularly those undergoing their National Service. Referring to the post-war aspiration for improved living standards, the history noted that 'the good name of the RASC in the eyes of the military and the public came very much to depend, for its entire humble image, on the efficient performance of Barrack Services.'

Kathleen had petitioned for a divorce from her husband William, and the provisional order for the divorce (the decree nisi) was granted on the 14th July 1944. I do not know the details of the case, just that the document simply names Kathleen as the petitioner and William as the respondent - there is no reference to a co-respondent. The decree nisi was then made absolute on the 22nd January 1945 and this enabled William to remarry later that year, in October. Kathleen, however, had to wait until after George's divorce was complete before she could remarry.

The law provided that divorce could be sought by either a husband or a wife on account of their spouse's adultery. However the law would not allow the divorce to proceed if there was found to be any evidence of collusion between the divorcing parties, although this did actually happen in many cases. I believe that it almost certainly happened in the case of George's divorce from Evelyn.

My understanding of the matter is that it was mutually agreed that the best way forward for those involved was for Evelyn to seek a divorce from George on account of his adultery with Kathleen. Therefore, in order to satisfy the requirements of the divorce laws, George and Kathleen would have to travel to a town such as Brighton, which was popularly associated with what had become known as the 'divorce racket'. Here they could provide the 'evidence' for the divorce by allowing themselves to be seen in a hotel bedroom together. All that would be needed would be for them to be seen by a witness such as a hotel room-maid. Alternatively a hotel bill, showing their joint occupation of a room, could also be used as evidence of adultery. Once they had been 'caught' in one or other of these circumstances at the hotel, the resulting evidence would have allowed Evelyn to petition for divorce from George.

The records indicate that Evelyn petitioned for divorce on 14th November 1945 and that the decree absolute was granted on the 20th May 1946. This meant that George and Kathleen were now free to marry, and they did so just over a month later on the 22nd June 1946 at the Register Office in Salisbury, some nine miles from Kathleen's Amesbury home. One witness was Kathleen's mother Rose Williams, while the other was Dorothy Daykin who had originally helped to bring George and Kathleen together. After the wedding, George returned to Chester before a brief posting to No 2 Holding Battalion RASC at Thetford in Norfolk.

Meanwhile Kathleen and Valerie remained in Amesbury, where Kathleen started the process of changing Valerie's surname by deed poll from Wiltshire to Gaunt. This was completed on the 12th September and was an act that Valerie found to be most distressing. The overnight change of name was a very difficult matter for a six-year-old to try and explain to her school-friends; particularly at a time when divorce was still widely regarded as being socially unacceptable.

Although George maintained contact with Evelyn, Kathleen had made a much cleaner break with William. When the marriage had first started to break down, Kathleen had allowed Valerie to have limited contact with her father, but after this time she was not permitted any further contact with him at all.

The stay in Thetford for George was followed by a posting to Gibraltar, which he reached by ship on the 6th October 1946 and then served with 33 Company RASC. This was a Motor Transport unit based at New Mole Barracks, and George was responsible for the stores and stores accounts of Barrack Services. No 33 Company was an important provider of road transport on Gibraltar, having four platoons of vehicles, including both Jeeps and various tippers. One of the Company's key tasks was to supply drivers for the Royal Engineers working in the numerous tunnels that honeycombed the towering Rock of Gibraltar. It also provided support services for the Gibraltar Garrison, which, according to the RASC History, consisted of 'two or three regiments of Artillery, one or two battalions of Infantry, substantial numbers of engineers, a large Air Force contingent and a sizeable Naval presence in the large Government Dockyard'.

The Quarterly Historical Record for the Company in 1946 complained that 'replacement drivers from the UK are frequently found not to be experienced and up to the standard'. These troops apparently required 'additional instruction', although the report did acknowledge that 'this can be understood when the difficulty of tricky and narrow roadways are taken into account'. The report went on to record that 'The morale of troops in the unit is of a fairly high level, when it is realized how boring such a compact place as the 'Rock' can be'.

It is likely that a contributing factor to this problem was also the Army's conversion from a war footing to a peacetime force, because many experienced soldiers were being replaced by less experienced National Servicemen. This was partly acknowledged in a report on the performance of the company in 1947, which noted that 'The functioning of this unit has been made rather difficult by such factors as the aged condition of many vehicles, the steady turnover of personnel and the heavy demands made on the unit'. The RASC had moved out of Gibraltar by 1963, and New Mole Barracks later became the headquarters of the Gibraltar Police.

When he was first in 'Gib', as Gibraltar was commonly called, George shared a bungalow known as New Aloes in Europa Road with various other officers who were well looked after by a Spanish servant called 'Wanna'. Amongst the officers was Major Frank Ayre of the Royal Engineers, who later wrote in a letter of reference that George was 'scrupulously honest and trustworthy, of temperate habits, always cheerful and of a pleasant disposition. He is hard working himself and able to bring out the best in those placed in his charge. To his military superiors I always found him respectful without any trace of loss of his own self-respect.' Frank concluded his reference by saying that George was 'a well-balanced person and a good 'mixer' and I count myself fortunate to have known him.' Researching information relating to New Aloes on the Internet revealed that, after a controversial sale in 2004, the building had been subsequently demolished and the site redeveloped.

George's posting to Gib meant that he was not only living in a warm climate and with the benefit of a servant but that he was fortunate enough to avoid England's terrible winter of 1946/47. The severe cold spell began towards the end of January 1947, with blizzards and freezing temperatures heralding a lengthy period without sun. Snow was often piled up in drifts of ten feet or more, resulting in the widespread closure of roads and railways. During this time Kathleen and Valerie were still living with Kathleen's parents in Amesbury, where fir trees were close to the house, and Valerie clearly remembered 'the awful cracking noise of the icicles on the trees banging together in the wind'. She also recalled that the house still had its war-time black-out curtains which supplemented the thick, fringed winter curtains and helped to keep out the drafts. The family would huddle around the kitchen stove for warmth, and beds were warmed at night with round stone water bottles. The use of the thick winter curtains would later be exchanged for bright cotton 'summer curtains' as the weather warmed.

At some point shortly thereafter, probably during the

middle part of 1947, Kathleen disposed of her business interests in Bulford, removed Valerie from her school in Amesbury and sailed to join George in Gibraltar. Once there, they moved with him into 10 Library Gardens, from where Valerie was sent to attend St George's Service School. This move to a sunnier climate must at least have had its compensations for both Kathleen and Valerie. August 1947 saw trips to the beach at Catalan Bay on the eastern side of Gibraltar, and to Getares in Spain which is on the opposite side of Gibraltar's bay. The warmth and the sunshine which they were now enjoying would have helped banish memories of the awful winter they had experienced.

During the time he was serving in Gibraltar George joined the Freemasons, being initiated into the United Services Lodge on the 16th October 1947 and serving as Lodge Steward for the year 1947/48. This lodge had been founded in 1923 for members of all ranks in the three armed services stationed on the Rock of Gibraltar, and I imagine that George joined because it was expected of officers at the time. Freemasons trace their origins to the guilds, or lodges, of working masons in the middle ages who recognised their fellow craftsmen by secret signs. By the 17th Century these lodges had largely ceased to have any direct connection with the mason's trade, and in 1717 four of the lodges in London came together and united to form a 'grand lodge', from which the present Grand Lodge of England is directly descended. This united lodge had a new constitution and a new objective of mutual help and fellowship. Signs of the lodge's origins continue however in the use of old Masonic symbols and ritual. The London Grand

Lodge then became the parent of other lodges, both in Britain and around the world.

The end of George's tour of duty in Gibraltar saw the family return to the UK on the 11th April 1948 and, on the 16th of that month, George was stationed at Shrivenham, where he was Assistant Officer in Charge of Barracks. On 26th July he was posted to Le Marchant Barracks at Devizes in Wiltshire, where he was Officer in Charge of Barracks. Kathleen's family had connections with these barracks, because her father had joined the Wiltshire Regiment there as a 14-year-old boy soldier in 1894, and his father, Patrick Williams, had been the Barrack Sergeant there at the time. It is possible that Patrick's job could have been broadly comparable to the duties later carried out by George. It is likely that George's assignments in both Shrivenham and Devizes will also have been broadly similar, being involved with the provision and management of accommodation and stores, and for arranging the supply of various fuel types such as gas, water and electricity for the Barracks. During this time, while George was away on these postings, Kathleen and Valerie moved back to live with Kathleen's parents in Amesbury.

Towards the latter part of 1948, George's RASC duties took him to the War Office (now the Ministry of Defence) in London, where the office of the Quarter Master General (QMG) was responsible for the central administration of RASC operational issues. This posting provided a different working environment to that which George had been used to in the past, and he was able to wear civilian clothes rather than military uniform. At about this time, on the 22nd October, he also took the opportunity to become a Life Member of the London Branch of the Old Coldstreamers Association. I still have his membership card in my possession.

George obviously needed to live within reasonable commuting distance of the job, and so, with Kathleen and Valerie, he moved to the London suburb of Ealing. There he rented a two-bedroom fully furnished flat on the first floor of 48 Connell Crescent. This was a comparatively modern property dating from the 1930s, which from the street looked just like an ordinary semi-detached house. The flat was close to Park Royal tube station, and therefore convenient for daily travel to central London. However Valerie, whose ninth birthday fell on the 1st January 1949, had to catch a bus to her new school.

Some 52 years later, in 2001, a new generation of the Gaunt family would renew the connection with the Ealing locality when my son Stuart moved there to attend Thames Valley University. This is located near to the centre of the town and close to the famous Ealing Film Studios. While waiting to meet Stuart one day, Shirley and I took the opportunity to take the short train ride to visit Connell Crescent and see the flat where Dad, Mum and Valerie had lived. It's still there, and the street appeared to be largely unchanged apart, perhaps, from the almost solid rows of cars parked along both sides of the road and the greatly increased roar of traffic from nearby Western Avenue.

The flat appears to have been only a stopgap measure while more permanent accommodation could be found, and Valerie recalls being taken on a number of trips to see the construction of a bungalow which was planned as the family's new home.

However this was located much closer to the centre of London than was Ealing, and Kathleen eventually decided that living there was not for her. It would therefore appear that she then successfully persuaded George to resign from the Army. His records show that he was granted a period of leave from the 30th November 1948, which he spent at Amesbury, and that he was then released from military service on the 28th February 1949 at the age of 45.

George's service in the Army meant that he was presented with the following Medals: The General Service Medal 1918-1962, with the clasp 'Palestine' for service in that country, and which is engraved on the edge with his Coldstream Guards number, rank and name; The Defence Medal, awarded for the defence of Britain during a time of threatened enemy invasion and heavy air attacks; The 1939-45 War Medal, which is the standard medal for the Second World War; and the Regular Army Long Service and Good Conduct Medal, which is engraved on the edge with his Army Air Corps number, name and rank. He was also awarded the 'King's Badge', which bears the inscription 'For Loyal Service'.

While George's leaving the Army may seem to be a particularly momentous event, I'm not at all sure that this was entirely the case. He had been in the Army for 24 years, serving in peacetime and in wartime, in élite units and in support units, and he had risen through the ranks to be eventually commissioned as an officer. Essentially he had probably achieved as much as was possible in his Army career, so he may well have been ready for a change. It is also worth noting that Army life was not always easy for his family, who frequently took second place to soldiering. They were so often on the move, with little chance of a settled home life, which could be very hard, particularly where children were concerned. We have already seen how George's first family was carted around the country from posting to posting, having to live with relatives, or in rented accommodation, or in temporary Army housing. Even in his comparatively short time as an officer with the RASC, he had already been moved around quite considerably, with the consequent separation from his new family, which he was finding most difficult; and there was probably no guarantee that the posting to the War Office in London would not soon be followed by yet another move somewhere else.

Following his release from the Army, George soon secured a job as a Stores Manager and part-time Relief Cinema Manager on the Isle of Wight. Moving from London in readiness to start his new job on the 14th April, George, Kathleen and Valerie initially lodged with Mrs Vanner at No 28 West Street in Ryde. It was while she was living here that Kathleen refined her cooking skills, with Mrs Vanner's help and guidance, to become an absolutely wonderful cook with a richly deserved reputation for making melt-in-your-mouth pastry that one could only dream about.

I'm not entirely certain how the job on the Isle of Wight came about, but it may have been through George's Army connections, because he was employed by Southern Cinemas Ltd. This company managed various cinemas/theatres across the south of England; its Chairman and Joint Managing Director was Lt Colonel FCR Britten. He was formerly of the

Coldstream Guards, and although he and George had never served in the same Battalion, Lt Col Britten wrote 'I always heard very good reports of him'. It could well have been these 'good reports' which helped George secure his job with the company.

Southern Cinemas had its administrative offices at the Commodore Theatre in George Street, Ryde, the largest town on the Island. The Commodore Theatre was opened in 1936 with a seating capacity of 1,507 and, in addition to providing a home for the company's general administrative offices, it operated both as a cinema and as a theatre, having full stage facilities as well as a café and ballroom. New films likely to have been among those screened at the Commodore that year were the Ealing comedy *Passport to Pimlico*, John Wayne's cavalry western *She Wore a Yellow Ribbon*, *Twelve O'clock High*, starring Gregory Peck, the Oscar-winning *Little Women*, based on the book by Louisa May Alcott, and *The Third Man*, famous for its haunting zither music, and starring Orson Welles.

George's job of Stores Manager was an echo of his earlier duties with the RASC in Gibraltar, because it also included the checking of all stores and accounts, although in this case they came from theatres and cinemas rather than military units. Lt Colonel Britten wrote that he was 'most efficient' in this task. George was also 'able to effect considerable economies and succeeded in cutting out much unnecessary paper work for the Theatre Managers'. At the same time he wrote that George 'maintained a high degree of control over the purchases and distribution of stores, amounting to many thousands of pounds every year.'

Not long after moving to the Island, George and Kathleen were walking along the street in Ryde when they were seen by a policeman on point duty. Waving on the traffic, he came over and, much to the surprise of them both, smartly saluted and introduced himself as Arthur Meadows, a former member of the Coldstream Guards. It was from this previous service that Arthur had recognised George as he walked up the street. Arthur then invited George and Kathleen to meet his wife Kaye and family who lived about three miles away in St Helens, where he was the village policeman.

After a move from Mrs Vanner's lodgings to a nearby top floor flat in another property, George, Kathleen and Valerie finally moved to settle in St Helens, living in a three bedroom semi-detached house named Sun Cottage, a short distance from Arthur Meadows' home at the police house in Station Road. It may also have been around this time that George obtained the first car I know about, which was a small dark-coloured Austin saloon with a registration number BUW 683. However I don't know when he learned to drive; it may have been while he was in the Army or it may have been while he was there on the Isle of Wight.

Sun Cottage was close to St Helens' large village green, as well as nearby open countryside, which meant there was plenty of room to exercise the golden-haired Labrador which George obtained. The dog was named Chota, which is the Hindi word for 'small measure', so it was a name almost certainly coined by George and taken from his Indian service during 1941/42. The house was rented from a poultry farmer named Wade who lived next door, and whose chicken-runs were spread across the ground immediately to the rear of Sun Cottage. Notwithstanding its name, Valerie remembered that the house was dark and cold, particularly in the winter.

This move also involved a change of schools for Valerie, who had to transfer from Ryde Junior School to St Helens County Junior School. However, despite the job on Isle of Wight getting them out of London, it became clear that Kathleen was not entirely happy living on the island, so the move failed to provide the permanence which I think both she and George had been seeking.

As their home was so close to the seaside, it did allow George and Kathleen the opportunity to receive family and friends on holiday visits to the island, and many did indeed come to stay. Family snapshots show visits from George's sister Flo and her husband Walter Ross, with their children Peggy and Andrew. Kathleen's sister, Marjorie Jones, together with Myfanwy and David, were also amongst the welcome visitors. Richard, however, was absent, because he had to remain with his unit. Other visitors included Frank Ayre, with whom George had worked in Gibraltar, who came to the island with his wife Lena and son, also named David.

Although Kathleen was mainly content during the summer months, and was able to entertain visitors during this time, she did feel very much isolated from her parents in Wiltshire during the winter. This was especially so when the ferry services were disrupted by bad weather. Kathleen was very attached to her parents, and her feelings of isolation must have become even more acute following the death of her father in May 1950, although her mother had later been able to visit them on the island. Perhaps George could relate to this attachment because he had, I think, been equally devoted to his own mother. He was to develop a similarly close relationship with Kathleen's mum, whom he and Kathleen always knew as 'Mother'. Accordingly he agreed that they should move once again, this time back to the mainland, and that he should seek a job nearer to her home.

The resulting search for yet another job was probably under way as early as January 1951, because George received two letters of reference during that month. The first was from Major Frank Ayre, and has already been quoted, while the second was provided by Major F R Hoxey MBE of the Royal Artillery. Major Hoxey explained that he had known George since making his acquaintance in 1945. He wrote that George 'has always been a very keen worker and an energetic participant in all his undertakings, whether at work or recreation. He is outstanding and smart in personal appearance, and of temperate habits. His main object appears to be able to perform his duties in such a manner not only to the satisfaction of his superiors but beneficial to all concerned in whatever undertaking is being carried out.' Major Hoxey further wrote 'I can thoroughly recommend him for a position of trust and responsibility in any civilian public service.'

While receipt of these letters did not herald an immediate move, George's circumstances did change later in the year when he secured a job working at the Salisbury Plain District Officers' Mess of the Army's Southern Command, located in the Beacon Barracks complex at Bulford Camp. Of course it was while George had been stationed at Bulford Camp in 1943 that he and Kathleen had first met, so they were both familiar with the area. While I understand that George and Kathleen must have been seeking a return to the mainland for some time, the actual event, when it finally happened, came about quite suddenly. Valerie had only just passed her 11-plus exam and was preparing to attend Sandown Grammar School. Her school uniform had even been purchased, but she never had an opportunity to wear it before the family moved back to the mainland.

George left his employment with Southern Cinemas on the 15th September 1951 and, in a glowing letter of reference which has already been partly quoted, Lt Colonel Britten confirmed that George was leaving his job on the Island in order 'to take up an appointment near his own home'. Lt Colonel Britten then went on to write ' I am very sorry to lose him and will always be only too glad to recommend him with every confidence for a post of responsibility, and where his administrative capabilities could be made full use of.' Despite the resulting move away from the Island, the friendship with Arthur and Kaye Meadows endured, and many happy family holidays were subsequently spent with them.

An advantage with the job in the officers' mess was that accommodation was provided, which saved George from the complication of having to look both for a new job and for somewhere to live at the same time. This was additionally advantageous because he seems to have disposed of the little Austin which he had used on the Isle of Wight, possibly because he didn't need a car at this time. He could also have had to take into account the expense involved in running a car, because I think he may still have been sending money to his former family. Bernard certainly remembers that, long after he had left home and joined the Coldstream Guards, he was approached by a Guards Sergeant who brought him a ten shilling (50 pence) note, saying 'this is from your Dad'. But Bernard still wanted nothing to do with his father, having been too wounded by his treatment of him, so he would not accept the money and told the Sergeant to take it away.

Having left the Isle of Wight, George, Kathleen and Valerie briefly stayed with Kathleen's Mother in Amesbury before moving into the Steward's Quarters for the Officer's Mess. At this time the family still had their dog Chota with them, but he was sadly to die shortly afterwards from distemper.

The mess where George was employed is a grand brick-built building with a colonnaded entrance, situated at the junction of Plumer Road (later renamed Wyvern Road) and Headquarters Street at the south eastern edge of the camp. I was very kindly given a tour of its facilities in April 2012 by RQMS Alex George, whose 1st Battalion Royal Anglian Regiment now occupies the building as the unit's sergeants' mess. Ground floor accommodation consists of ante-room, bar area and a magnificent dining room, together with various rest and recreation rooms, while bedrooms occupy the first floor.

The mess was also very close to the home of Frank and Peggy Etwell in the adjacent housing known as Messines Lines, subsequently demolished. Frank worked in the Barracks Stores Department, while Peggy had managed one of Kathleen's shops for her in the Garrison Market during the early 1940s, so they may have played a part in helping George gain his job at the Mess. Alternatively the job may have come to him through his various Army contacts. The steward's quarters consisted of a small, square, brick-built two-bedroom bungalow in the grassed-over grounds of the mess. A large rebuilding programme had started at Bulford Camp in 1932 when the old wooden barracks were replaced by permanent brick buildings; and it seems that the officers' mess and the adjacent bungalow were built during this period. They are not shown on the 1928 Ordnance Survey map of the camp, but do appear on the 1939 edition

Valerie was now sent to school in Durrington, but she did not settle there at all, so George and Kathleen removed her and sent her to Amesbury High School, where she stayed for only a matter of weeks before going on to the South Wilts Grammar School for Girls in Salisbury. Her journey to and from this particular school was a long one, which started each morning with a 20-minute walk from the bungalow to the bus stop on the Amesbury Road, where she had to catch the Wilts & Dorset bus to Salisbury. During these journeys she met Jill Warner, who also lived on the camp and who travelled the same route each day to Salisbury High School. They became firm friends during these trips and happily remain so to this day.

Although the move to Bulford had achieved the desirable aim of being closer to Kathleen's mother, as well as securing for George an important post, the living accommodation may not have been ideal. The bungalow was very small, and I thought it most claustrophobic for a family home when I was given the opportunity to look it over in 2012. It was also lacking in privacy because it didn't have any garden land of its own.

The Book of Mess Management states: 'The Commanding Officer is responsible for the management, discipline and general well-being of the mess. He may at his discretion, delegate such responsibilities and duties in connection with the management and discipline of the mess as he wishes to a Mess Management Committee, but he remains ultimately responsible for its general conduct, tone and management.' George recorded his job title as 'Mess Steward', so he will have worked under the direction of the Mess Management Committee President, who will, I imagine, have considered him ideally suited for this task.

He had the references provided by Majors Ayre and Hoxey and which, quoted earlier, seem almost tailor-made for this particular job. He also had the benefit of considerable expertise derived from his work with the RASC and Southern Cinemas, which will have added to his suitability for the post. Finally, his background in the Coldstream Guards will also have served him well. For example, and to quote again from the Book of Mess Management: 'The Officers' Mess is the home of all living-in officers, and the club for all serving officers. It is also the centre of social life, and as such, it must at all times be maintained at the highest possible degree of efficiency and cleanliness. The very high standard demanded can only be achieved and maintained by the efficiency and excellence of the staff that it employs. It is therefore imperative that the staff are personnel of the highest integrity whose discipline, deportment, personal cleanliness and courtesy are at all times beyond reproach.' Reading these notes reminded me very much of the high standards detailed as requirements in the

'Notes for Lecturers' at the Caterham Guards Depot, which I believe underpinned the whole of George's Army service.

Amongst his various duties, which included 'the general day-to-day running of the Officers Mess', he was also responsible for the supervision of daily messing and preparation of menus, the purchase of additional foodstuffs, the allocation of accommodation to officers living in, the supervision of the cleanliness of the mess generally and the supervision of cellar and bar stocks. He will additionally have been charged with making the arrangements for regimental dinners, guest nights and other social or official entertainment. Certainly Valerie spoke of him supervising big important dinners, and remembers seeing the tables laid out with starched white table cloths and the mess silverware. She also recalls two staff who were apparently Czechoslovakian, and possibly WW2 refugees. They will have been working under George's direct supervision and, according to the Book of Mess Management, will have been 'responsible for the cleanliness of the mess, valeting for living in officers, waiting at tables and such other duties as are required for the general well-being of the mess'.

It was during this time in Bulford that I was born, some 12 miles away at the Harnham Croft Nursing Home in Harnham Road, Salisbury, on the 6th May 1952. I remember being told that the period following my birth was a rather difficult time because I was apparently quite a poorly baby; I couldn't swallow my milk and was constantly sick. The doctors seemed to think I had some form of digestive system blockage, but the problem was eventually resolved and I was allowed home. My baptism took place on the 7th September at the nearby Bulford Garrison Church of St George, which Dad and Mum attended and where Valerie sang in the choir. My godparents were Frank and Lena Ayre, together with Frank Etwell.

August 1953 saw an important event for Valerie when her confirmation service was held. This was conducted in the magnificent surroundings of Salisbury Cathedral on the 6th August by the Lord Bishop of Salisbury, William Sarum. Jill Warner was confirmed at the same time, and Valerie remembered how 'awe-inspiring' it was as the two girls stood outside the cathedral in their white confirmation dresses waiting to go in for the service.

1953 was another year of change for the family, because Dad next secured an appointment as Licensee of the Eliot Arms public house in the village of South Cerney in Gloucestershire. The village is close to the Gloucestershire/Wiltshire border and about four miles from Cirencester. Dad very likely secured this job as a result of his contacts with Messrs H & G Simonds of Reading, who had a long history of close connections with the Army, and almost certainly supplied the drinks to the officers' mess from their Salisbury Plain depot about nine miles from Bulford in Tidworth Road, Ludgershall.

Simonds had probably secured the contract to supply the mess as a result of their links with the Army, which were recognised as extensive and well-established. For example a 1960 history of Simonds noted that 'From its earliest days there has always been a close connection between the firm and the armed services. Wherever the British Army went, Simonds beer went too'. Indeed, Simonds' links with the Army on Salisbury Plain pre-date the building of the permanent barracks there and can be traced back as far as the summer manoeuvres on the Plain in 1872.

This connection with Simonds would also explain Dad's move from Bulford to South Cerney, a village some 45 miles away and with no obvious family link. His successful work in the mess could easily have led him to consider moving on to become a pub landlord, where he would be his own boss. Such a move would have the additional advantage of allowing Mum to be involved in some way with the work of the pub. Thus, if Simonds were supplying the drinks to the mess, they would be the obvious firm to turn to for advice on this matter. Having seen the bungalow for myself, I am also convinced that neither Mum nor Dad would have been very happy or comfortable living there permanently, particularly with a young family, so that situation must have seriously influenced their decision to move on. If Dad then discussed the possibility of a job change with Simonds, they could have suggested that he might consider taking over at the Eliot Arms, where the existing Licensee was planning to leave. This is the only way I can explain Dad seeking a job with a Berkshire-based brewer in a Gloucestershire village rather than, for example, approaching any of the nearer Wiltshire Brewers such as Gibbs Mew in Salisbury or Wadworths in Devizes.

Valerie found out about the move in a rather strange way. Following their respective confirmations, she and Jill had gone to stay for a week with Flo and Walter Ross in Beeston. Returning to Wiltshire by Black & White Coach at the end of the holiday, they passed through Cirencester during the late afternoon. Shortly afterwards the coach stopped, apparently in the middle of nowhere. Much to the surprise of Valerie and Jill, Dad and Mum climbed aboard for the remainder of the journey home. The coach had, in fact, stopped at a bus stop about 1½ - 2 miles north-east of the village at the end of Northmoor Lane, where it joined the old Cirencester to Swindon road next to the airfield of RAF South Cerney.

Apart from the surprise of their arrival, Dad and Mum brought news that the family were moving to live in South Cerney. Appalled at the prospect of the upheaval and losing her friends, Valerie told me that her diary for the day clearly recorded that she really didn't want to go to 'South Surney'. This was an entirely understandable point of view because, although only 13 years of age, Valerie had already attended some nine different schools, with all the trauma and upheaval such changes must entail. She said later that she had never been at a particular school long enough to properly make friends, which was why, of course, she was so horrified at the possibility of losing touch with her best friend Jill when told of the latest move.

Noting that Dad and Mum had travelled back to Wiltshire on the coach, I set about trying to work out how they could have journeyed up to South Cerney from Bulford in the first place. Clearly it couldn't have been by car, or they wouldn't have needed to return on the coach; it must have been by public transport. Nonetheless a bus journey would have been extremely arduous, because they would probably have had to change at Marlborough and would certainly have had to change at Swindon. Even then there was only a bus every two hours from Swindon direct to South Cerney, so making the appropriate connections could have been very difficult indeed, if not impossible.

However, researching the history of the railway in South Cerney on the Internet, I discovered that a train journey, on the other hand, was quite simple and straightforward. The September 1953 timetable for the British Rail Western Region Andover-Cheltenham line shows an 07.50 departure on the branch line from Tidworth to Ludgershall, Tidworth being the next village to Bulford. From Ludgershall Dad and Mum could have caught the 08.07, which would take them through various country stations such as Marlborough (08.46), Swindon Town (09.13) and Cricklade (09.32), to South Cerney, arriving at 09.40. Alternatively, a short taxi journey, or lift from a friend, could take them straight to Ludgershall to catch the train from there. Either way this would give them plenty of time in South Cerney to view the pub and then walk the two miles, or be given a lift, to the end of Northmoor Lane in time to catch the coach back home in the afternoon.

The Bulford bungalow apparently remained unoccupied after we had all moved out, and does not appear to have been lived in again for some considerable time. Valerie actually saw it in use as a store when she visited the area with Jill some years later. By 2012 the bungalow was being used as overflow accommodation for the sergeants' mess. Apart from the conversion of the bathroom into a separate shower room and toilet, it was otherwise remarkably unchanged from Mum and Dad's time.

CHAPTER SIX

A VILLAGE INNKEEPER

'Beer is living proof that God loves us and wants us to be happy.' -
Benjamin Franklin

Dad, Mum, Valerie and I moved to live at the Eliot Arms in
October 1953 where, just short of his 50th birthday, Dad
embarked on a fresh career as a pub licensee, a job which
proved indeed to be a natural progression from his previous
work in the officers' mess at Bulford. The transfer of the licence
from the pub's previous licensee, Mr N C Richards, who had
been there since March 1948, was later reported in the local
newspaper as having been given final approval at a sitting of
the Cirencester Magistrates on Wednesday 11th November.

Becoming a licensee was a favoured job for ex-servicemen
during the 1950s, and many of Dad's contemporaries in the
licensed trade around Cirencester were similarly old soldiers,
noticeably including a profusion of former NCOs. Valerie's
objections to the move had clearly fallen on deaf ears and once
again (although happily for the last time), she had to endure a
change of school, exchanging the Girl's Grammar School in
Salisbury for the Grammar School in Cirencester, to which

she travelled each day on the green liveried buses of Bristol Tramways (renamed the Bristol Omnibus Company in 1957).

Although South Cerney was obviously further away from Amesbury than Bulford had been, it was much more straightforward to get there than it had been from the Isle of Wight, so contact with Mum's family could be readily maintained. Settling in the village would also bring an end to Dad and Mum's various wanderings since Dad had left the Army four years previously. South Cerney was a large village, even in those days, with a 1951 population of 1,942 served by three pubs, the other two being the Old George Inn, situated opposite the Eliot Arms and owned by West Country Brewers and the Royal Oak, located towards the southern end of the village. Both the Eliot Arms and the Royal Oak were owned by Simonds, who had acquired them in 1937, along with 90 other pubs, when they took over the Cirencester Brewery Company. The village was also well provided for in respect of various shops, garages and local services as well as being on the local bus route in addition, of course, to having its own railway station.

The station was opened in 1883 and formed part of an ambitious plan to provide a direct rail link between Birmingham and Southampton through Cheltenham via the Midland & South Western Junction Railway. However the scheme never really achieved its aims and the company was subsequently absorbed by the GWR in 1923. The station and the rest of the line then regrettably fell victim to the 'Beeching Axe' and closed firstly to passengers in 1961, then to goods traffic in 1963. Apart from this particular journey, I don't think either Dad or Mum ever used the station again or certainly not to any great extent, preferring instead to use the car. Of course it was lack of patronage such as this which goes some way to explaining the station's demise. Indeed I can only ever remember one subsequent use of the station, and that was when Ken Meadows, the eldest son of Arthur and Kaye Meadows, had been staying with us and Dad took him to the station to catch a train from there back to his home on the Isle of Wight.

The Eliot Arms was very different from the modern hotel it is today. It was then an east-facing three-storey semi-detached Cotswold stone and stone-tile built property in the middle of the village and close to the River Churn. The 1863 tithe map for the village, although not entirely clear, does appear to indicate a vacant plot where the Eliot Arms now stands. This would support the view that the pub was built somewhat later and that it probably dates from about 1870/1871, being first mentioned in a deed of 30th December 1871 when Robert Stanton sold it to Messrs Cripps & Co of the Cirencester Brewery. At that time it was described as 'that newly erected dwelling-house and inn called The Eliot Arms with barn, stables, outbuildings and yard, and also the cottage with pieces of ground on east and west'.

The first census entry for the Eliot Arms that I could find also appeared in that year when the April 1871 Census recorded George Woodward as the pub's licensee. The Eliot Arms had apparently not changed a great deal over the years when an entry in the H & G Simonds' Estates History Ledger for 1948 described it as 'A high three-storey stone and stone building with butchers shop and garage adjoining'. The description also stated that the Eliot then had 'No water heating but main water and electric lighting. Bucket drainage'.

There are only three pubs in the country with the name of Eliot Arms, the others being at St Germans and Tregadillett, both in Cornwall. Eliot is the family name of the Cornish Earls of St Germans, whose coat of arms and family motto is shown on the pub sign. The motto, *Praecedentibus Insta*, means 'Press closely on those that take the lead'. The Eliot family home is at Port Eliot in St Germans, Cornwall, but in the late 18th Century they had purchased the Down Ampney estate, about four miles from South Cerney, which was used as a second seat and a shooting lodge. The Eliot family apparently also owned land in the South Cerney area, and it is this connection which may have led to the pub acquiring its name. There was also an Eliot Arms in Down Ampney village, which apparently closed at around the same time as the South Cerney one opened. Perhaps the name was transferred? The Down Ampney estate was eventually sold by the 7th Earl in 1929.

A low-roofed cottage, known as Eliot Cottage, housing the local butcher's shop and associated greengrocers, was attached to one side. It seems that this property had originally been occupied together with the pub, because George Woodward's occupation was described in all the censuses from 1871 to 1901 as being variously 'Licensed Victualler' or 'Innkeeper' and each occupation then linked with the additional occupation of 'Butcher.' However the butcher's shop and cottage was now in separate occupancy. The tenant was Mr Charles F Mate, a master butcher, who had been in the cottage since at least 1934. An agreement between him and the

Cirencester Brewery Co in that year required him 'To keep the interior of the premises in good and tenantable repair and so deliver up'. By 1954 Mr Mate had offered to buy the shop and dwelling for £450, but this offer was rejected by Simonds, who were stated to be 'not interested in selling at a figure less than £1200'. However negotiations continued, and a note in Simonds' Estates Ledger for the 6th April 1959 reported 'an offer of £700 for the Butchers Shop adjoining this house'. The note went on to recommend acceptance 'if the proposed purchaser is not prepared to increase his offer'.

There must have been further negotiations, because the shop and cottage were eventually sold, interestingly, to Mrs Ethel Mate rather than her husband Charles, on the 23rd May 1960 for £725. It must have been shortly afterwards that I remember Eliot Cottage being improved and extended by the provision of a new kitchen and a bathroom with an inside toilet. Charles Mate ceased trading in about 1968 or 1969, although the butcher's shop continued in use until 1994. The ownership of Eliot Cottage then turned full circle when it was sold to the owners of the Eliot Arms, and the former butcher's shop was used as a coffee lounge attached to the pub. Further alterations later incorporated the whole of the cottage into the Eliot Arms when it became a hotel.

On the southern side of the Eliot was Cecil Huxley's garage and petrol filling station. This was also owned by Simonds, who, in 1952, were renting the property to Mr Huxley at an annual rental of £40, paid monthly. It was described rather simply in the rental agreement as 'All that Garage and Office adjoining the Eliot Arms'. By December 1956 the Estates

History Ledger recorded that Simonds had 'received an offer of £675 for the Garage and forecourt attaching thereto, adjoining this house, from the tenant (Mr. Huxley). Recommended this offer be accepted'.

Cecil always finished work and closed his garage at 6 pm each weekday, just at the same time that the pub opened, and he would then come into the public bar for his regular drink of a bottle of brown ale before going home. As the pub had only just opened, he was usually the first customer of the evening so, as I grew older and under Dad or Mum's supervision, I was sometimes allowed to serve him and take the payment for the drink, learning how to deal with the complicated pre-decimal coinage of pounds, shillings and pence.

The Eliot had a gravel-surfaced car park to the front. This often provided a convenient base for the salute to be taken on Remembrance Sunday as the British Legion marched past on their way from the church to the war memorial at the southern end of the village. To the pub's rear was a yard surrounded by various outbuildings. These can be seen on the site layout plan (Plan 1). The beer store and adjoining skittle alley were located in the ground floor of an old Cotswold stone barn. A hatch had been created in the dividing wall between the two which could be opened up to provide a bar servery during skittles matches. Space was also made in the beer store for a barrel or barrels to be placed so that draught beer could be supplied to the skittles players. This saved them having to go back and forth across the yard with drinks from the main pub building.

Outside the skittle alley were wooden steps leading up to the barn's first floor. This consisted of a large central loft with two partitioned rooms at each end. The doorways to these rooms were blocked by pieces of timber, and I remember as a child being frightened to go into them because, with no light, they were very spooky. I was also told that I couldn't go into those rooms because the floors were said to be unsafe, but fear of the dark kept me out just as effectively. The central area was lit by a single electric light and low-level dirty windows, and was mostly empty, although it was used occasionally to store apples from the trees in the garden.

The soft drinks store and the coal shed were both of corrugated iron construction, as was the timber-panelled function room (known as 'the Hut'). The original, and disused, toilets adjoined the barn, while relatively new male and female toilets built of concrete blocks were situated between the barn/skittle alley and the main part of the pub.

Attached to the rear of Cecil's garage premises, and originally forming a single property with it, was the place where Dad kept his car. This large building was constructed of concrete blocks and corrugated iron on a metal frame and probably dated from the early years of the 20th century, when the Eliot was occupied by Harry Gigg, who used it as his workshop. Harry was described on the 1911 Census as a 'Coachbuilder' working at home on his 'own account,' but the census entry makes no mention of him being a licensee. Harry's son is also described as a 'coachbuilder' but there are no employment descriptions for his wife or daughter, so he presumably treated the pub business very much as a secondary occupation. The garden shed adjoining the car shelter on the far side was almost certainly a former stable.

There was a large garden immediately behind the outbuildings, separated from those buildings by a high stone wall which had presumably served as the Eliot's original rear boundary. The garden led in turn to a largely overgrown paddock with various fruit trees scattered around, and a pigsty at the far end. This paddock had been described in a 1929 Title Document as 'Pasture Land or Water Meadow' and was originally part of a much larger area of land known as 'Grettons' which is shown on the Tithe Map as running parallel to most of Clarks Hay and as far north as the River Churn. Much of this land now forms the site of Churn Close.

H & G Simonds Ltd had purchased the paddock in April 1948, along with the garden, from Sarah Jane Carpenter for £430. Mrs Carpenter was a former tenant at the pub, having taken over the tenancy in 1929 upon the death of her husband, Francis. She had then relinquished her tenancy in March 1948 at about the same time as the sale of the land to Simonds was completed. The garden and paddock were bounded on the southern and western sides by a tall yew hedge and on the northern side by a tangled thicket of bushes stretching along the bank of the river.

The paddock was the subject of various purchase enquiries in 1958 but was not considered suitable for sale on its own because the only access was through the pub garden. However, some alternative access must have been identified because an offer of £250 was made for the land in February 1959. Simonds then decided to accept this offer as the land was surplus to their requirements, although the deal had fallen through by August because the proposed purchaser had apparently been unable to obtain permission to secure appropriate access. The land was then described in the Estates Ledger as 'unsaleable'. This judgment was later shown to have been rather premature because, within a couple of years, access was provided from School Lane via a new bridge constructed over the River Churn and two bungalows (called 'Rananim' and 'Tangmere') were built on the land.

I was appalled at the decision to sell this land. At a single stroke, most of my playground was going to be taken away, and neither Mum nor Dad nor anyone else would listen to my increasingly desperate protestations.

With an unguarded river running beside the garden, the inevitable happened, and one day Polly Griffiths, an old lady whose cottage opposite the school in School Lane backed on to the river, came running to Dad and Mum shouting 'Your boy's in the river! Your boy's in the river!' Hurriedly rushing to the river, Dad expected to find me floating face down in the water. But it wasn't very deep, and he found me happily paddling along and totally unconcerned that my red wellington boots were full of water. I'm not sure what upset me most - being stopped from playing in the river or being told off for getting so wet.

The main entrance to the pub was through a central stone porch leading straight to a hatch for 'Off Sales'. A door to the left led into the public bar. Here the floor was tiled, and there was a dartboard in an alcove by the large open fireplace. A wooden settle (a long high-backed wooden bench seat) was placed against the rear wall of the bar, with additional seating on bare wooden chairs lined up along the tables opposite the settle. From the entrance porch, a door to the right led into the saloon bar, where the floor was carpeted and chairs were arranged in groups of four around small tables. In many pubs, the prices were a little higher in the saloon bar because of the (slightly) greater 'luxury', but I don't know if Dad applied this practice at the Eliot.

The rest of the ground floor accommodation consisted of a Kitchen, a private dining room and a sitting room, which also served as a breakfast room for overnight guests. This room had once been a bar-room and, in one wall, a serving hatch still existed. The wall at that point was thick enough for the disused hatch to act as an alcove, in which a television set was later placed. Access to this bar had originally been through a lean-to porch to the rear of the public bar but the doorway there had been blocked up thus forming a storage area. There was also a beer cellar where the barrels of beer were kept, and which partly extended under the adjoining shop premises at Eliot Cottage.

The accommodation on the first floor consisted of four private bedrooms and a bathroom/WC (which was shared with the guests). Dad and Mum's bedroom was on the right at the front, next to Eliot Cottage and above the saloon bar; my bedroom was the small, middle, room at the front while the bedroom to the left, above the public bar, was spare. Valerie's room was at the back overlooking the yard and above the sitting room.

My bedroom window was immediately above the porch entrance to the pub, and had a very wide window sill. This meant that I was able to sit on the sill and then climb out on to the porch roof - a highly dangerous undertaking for a child. Dad therefore had some wooden bars nailed across the window which, although rather unsightly, at least succeeded in keeping me inside and safe. These bars can just be seen on the March 1964 photograph of the pub, although by that time the room was empty because I had moved into Valerie's old room. Guest accommodation, consisting of a further four bedrooms, was located on the second floor at the top of the building. The room layout of the Eliot can be seen on the line plans (plans 2, 3 and 4).

The Eliot Arms was a 'tied house' which Dad rented from Simonds. Although Dad's tenancy details have not survived the passage of time, I have been able to ascertain the details regarding the furnishing of the pub. For example certain fixtures, such as the bar counters and the wooden settle along the wall of the public bar, were in the ownership of the brewery and formed part of the rental agreement and Dad would have been obliged to deposit a sum of money, called a 'Dilapidations Deposit', with the brewery to cover them. This deposit would then be used at the end of the tenancy to make good any defects or damages which might have occurred.

He would also have been required to buy the 'tenant's inventory' from Mr Richards on the day of change, together with any wet and dry stock in the pub on that day. This inventory would have included the furniture in the guest bedrooms which, in addition to bed, wardrobe and dressing table, consisted of old-fashioned, possibly Victorian, wooden wash-stands with a jug and basin for washing, together with a chamber pot under the bed. The use of these items had, however, been replaced by the later installation of the modern bathroom/WC shared with the family.

The inventory also included the furniture in the two bars which, in the saloon bar, consisted of a set of tables and chairs painted in light green that Valerie recalled as making it look more like a café than a pub. When the bar was later redecorated, these were replaced with dark wood tables and wheel-back chairs with red leather seats. Apart from acquiring this pub furniture, Dad and Mum also brought their own with them which had mostly been purchased on the Isle of Wight and included the family's bedroom pieces. However the Eliot was bigger than their previous homes, so additional furniture was purchased in Cirencester at the Dyer Street warehouse of Ovens Furnishing & Removals.

With tied houses the beer is supplied by the owning brewery whereas free houses are owned by the licensee and can buy their beer from any brewery they choose. Simonds also arranged for the supply of all the pub's soft drinks and spirits. The soft drinks included those produced by Leese Ing and Company Ltd of Swindon, which eventually ceased trading in 1973 when they were taken over by Ace Soft Drinks.

Beer was delivered every Tuesday on a lorry from Simonds Depot in Swindon, and the draymen used to manhandle the wooden barrels (or casks) of beer into the cellar for storage. This was where Dad had to learn new skills relating to the keeping of the beer. The casks were lifted on to a long bench-like rack (stillage) where they were laid horizontally, with triangular wooden wedges jammed under the sides to hold them in place and tilted at a slight angle towards the front. This allowed the beer to settle. Laying the casks horizontally meant that the bung-hole (previously on the side of the barrel) was now on the top, and it was then pierced with a 'spile' which is a wooden peg or spigot, allowing the cask to be vented and air to enter. This started the process of secondary fermentation of the beer.

When the beer was ready to be 'drawn', a brass tap would be driven into the other bung-hole on the end of the cask and joined to tubes connecting the cask to the beer pumps on the counter in the saloon bar. The first pint to be drawn would invariably be cloudy and unsuitable, but after a few pulls the beer would be ready to serve. An H & G Simonds 1952 price list shows that a pint of XX Mild at 1/0d (5p) was the cheapest draught beer available, while India Pale Ale (IPA) cost 1/3d (6p) and Extra Brown Ale cost 1/7d (8p). These were all listed as public bar prices, so the saloon bar prices could have been a little higher. The beer was usually served in standard one-pint or half-pint dimpled glass beer mugs, very different from the beaker-style glasses used in pubs today.

Although the cask beer was kept in the cellar, the bottled beer was kept in the beer store across the yard at the rear of the main pub building and next to the skittle alley. They were delivered, and then stored, in large wooden crates which were later made of metal or aluminium. These beers would have included such items as Velvet Stout and Tavern Pale Ale at 1/2½d (about 6p) per half-bottle. Tavern Pale Ale was advertised in the local newspaper as 'the stronger ale at a lighter price', and was later rebranded as 'Tavern Export Ale'. Other bottled beers included S. B. Pale Ale, Berry Brown Ale and Luncheon Stout (all at 1/6d per bottle) (about 7½ p) and

Bulldog Pale Ale (at 1/8½d per half-bottle) (about 9p). Whiteways Whimple Medium-Sweet Cyder was also available at 7d per half-bottle (3p).

Every morning the numbers of bottles sold the previous night were counted and the appropriate replacements brought over in their crates stacked on a trolley. The bottles would then be placed on the shelves behind the bar while the empty crates were stacked by the alcove doorway leading into the rear of the public bar. On purchase, the bottled beer would generally be poured into an elegant fluted style glass (it was unheard of then to drink from a bottle) and the empty bottle put in the crate ready for returning to the beer store the following morning. I remember that all of these bottles were of brown glass, in contrast to the different coloured beer bottles now available.

This process of refilling the shelves was known as 'bottling up' and was recalled by my cousin, Andrew Ross, who was often allocated the job when staying at the Eliot on holiday. Andrew lived in Beeston and remembered his mum (Flo) 'putting me on the bus from Nottingham and Uncle George meeting me at Cirencester in his little car. What an adventure and what a relief when I spotted Uncle George waiting for me.' Andrew went on to recall that he was given a cloth to wipe the dust off the neck of the bottles, and had to arrange them on the shelves, always with the label facing outwards. 'When our jobs were finished we were rewarded with a bottle of pop and a packet of crisps. What joy!'

Clearly the requirement for neatness and order in relation to the display of the bottles was entirely in keeping with Dad's early background in the Coldstream Guards.

Dad was a great one for singing while he was working, and

I still have his rather battered songbook entitled *Songs that will live forever*, which is signed 'G E Gaunt Glider Pilot Depot August 1944'. Songs were particularly favoured in the morning during the process of 'bottling up' and readying the pub for opening time, and formed a sort of verbal version of 'whistle while you work'. He also encouraged me to sing along as well, although I'm not at all sure what the rest of the household thought of that idea. One of the songs we used to sing came from Dad's time in the Parachute Regiment, and was sung to the tune of 'John Brown's Body.' The song told the story of a paratrooper who 'jumped from 40,000 feet without a parachute' and included the chorus line 'Glory, glory what a helluva way to die'. However, Dad had very strict ideas about children using decent language and while he was happy for me to sing the song, he would never allow me to sing 'helluva way to die' so I had to sing the much more polite words 'heck of a way to die' instead.

Directly opposite the Eliot, on a small triangle of grass, is a mature blue cedar tree planted to commemorate the Silver Jubilee of King George V in 1935. Following his arrival, Dad quickly involved himself in village life and arranged for a local electrical company, Messrs Johnson & Harding, to illuminate this tree for the Christmas season - the first time this had ever happened. He also arranged with the Vicar for carols to be sung under the tree on Christmas Eve and issued a general invitation for villagers to attend and participate. This event was very successful, with a splendid response from many villagers who joined in the carol singing with the choir from the parish church. It is also worth noting that the village was generally quite dark at that time, the only street lighting being provided by a few scattered gas lamps, so the tree with all its lights would have really stood out, providing a bright beacon for the villagers, many of whom will have had to make their way to the occasion by torchlight.

At a time when one could be regarded by some as a 'newcomer' and still be barely accepted after many years in the village, this event is all the more remarkable for it being organised by Dad a mere two months after arriving in South Cerney. The success of this event is, I think, a good illustration of his outgoing personality and ability to readily make friends. This early venture into the activities of the village was followed on the 3rd February when the newspaper reported Mum joining the local Mothers' Union at an admission service held in the church. This process of settling in extended to the Old Coldstreamers' Association, where Dad's records from the Guards HQ show that he maintained his membership by joining the Gloucester Branch of the Association, becoming an approved member on the 8th April 1954.

During their first winter in the village, Mum and Dad quickly discovered that once the pubs had shut, at about 10 pm, there was virtually no activity in the village and an eerie quiet descended. Thus any sound carried quite easily, and the noise of the nearby River Churn as it surged noisily over the weir could be clearly heard in the Eliot, where it often kept them awake. This was partly due to their bedroom lacking any form of soundproofing and being the nearest to the river, although separated from the river itself by Eliot Cottage.

The *Wilts and Gloucestershire Standard* for Saturday 10th July

1954 recorded the Annual General Meeting of South Cerney Football Club on the preceding Monday. Among the list of eighteen vice-presidents appointed at the meeting is the name of 'G. Gaunt', although the article doesn't explain why a village team should need quite so many vice presidents in addition to a committee of six, as well as a president and a chairman!

Christmas 1954 saw a repeat of the previous year's successful illumination of the Jubilee Tree opposite the Eliot, as noted in the newspaper 'through the kindness of Mr G Gaunt.' Again the lighting was provided by Messrs Johnson and Harding while, on Christmas Eve 'parishioners of all denominations gathered round to sing carols, led by the Vicar the Rev G Waddington-Jones and the Parish Choir.'

All three pubs in the village organised 'Thrift Clubs', where members paid in a certain amount of money, usually on a weekly basis, throughout the year which was then paid into a bank account. At the end of the year, generally just before Christmas, the club member would receive a payout in line with his or her weekly payments. I do not know precisely when the club at the Eliot began, but it is possible that Dad started the club after he became landlord. The first mention of a Thrift Club at the Eliot occurred in the local newspaper for the 8th January 1955, which announced that 'the first pay in for the year for members' would be on that Friday. Pay-in sessions and meetings of the Thrift Club committee were held in the 'Hut' and the appointment of the club's Officers and Committee was recorded in the newspaper of the 31st December 1955. They were listed as: President, Mr F Parsloe; chairman, Mr J Bolton; treasurer, Mr G E Gaunt; secretary,

Mr C. Allaway; committee, Messrs E. Taylor, J Price, C J Merchant and F Agg. The first pay-in for 1956 was on Friday 6th January, although there is no record of the amounts which were paid in. However I have been told that it is probably not likely to have been much more than about two shillings (10 pence) or perhaps two shillings and sixpence (otherwise 2/6d, which was also known as half a crown, now 12½ pence).

An early foray into pub sports took place in March 1955, when Dad organised an open individual darts tournament which was held in the public bar, and which the newspaper reported as being 'most successful'. The tournament was won by Mr G. Savory, who defeated Mr C. Price in the final match. Mr Savory's prize was an inscribed tankard, which was presented to him some days later after it had been suitably inscribed. The success of the tournament must have generated a good amount of interest, because the paper in July further reported that a team from the Eliot had joined the Cirencester and District Darts League.

The 'Hut' was a useful building which, apart from serving as a covered playroom for me and being used in connection with the pub, could also, with Dad's permission, be utilised for general village events. South Cerney boasted a fine and well-used village hall in School Lane, which had been opened in 1925, having been converted from a disused tithe barn given to the village by Capt. E T Cripps MC of South Cerney Manor. However in cases where the hall may not have been an appropriate venue, or perhaps when it was already in use, the Hut at the Eliot Arms could be utilised.

One fascinating and rather controversial use of the Hut was as a polling station, although elections were generally held either in the village hall or the school. However the Parish Council meeting in May 1955 heard a complaint 'as to why the Parish Council elections should be held at public expense in the Eliot Arms Hut instead of the school which would be free.' The complainant further noted that 'Many people do not like going on to licensed premises to vote and the elections could be fitted in with a teacher's rest day when the school would be closed.' Responding to the complaint, the council pointed out that it had 'nothing to do with the arrangement of the elections' which was explained to be the job of the Clerk to the Cirencester Rural District Council.

The hiring of the Hut in this case will almost certainly have been arranged with Dad. As the pub's tenant he will have been seeking to maximise his income from the business, so will have agreed an appropriate fee with the Election Officer. If a few voters, having fulfilled their civic duty, stopped off for a quick lunchtime or evening pint, then so much the better!

I have tried to find out if the records of this hiring have survived, but sadly they have not, so we will never know the amount of the alleged 'public expense' in this case. However an example of an entirely different, and less controversial, use of the Hut can be found in November 1963 when the South Cerney COSY Club introduced a Chiropody Service which was held there. The COSY club had been started in 1958 by Mabel Waddington-Jones, the wife of the village's former vicar. It was an organisation for older people in the village, and the initials stood for 'Cerney Over Sixty Years'.

I think the early years at the Eliot Arms were not very easy for Dad, or Mum for that matter. Apart from Dad having to settle down to an entirely new career, with a markedly different way of life from that which he had previously known, Mum said that, in addition to providing for us in South Cerney, he was also sending money to help with his brother Lyn's business interests in Manchester. In any event, the early years at the pub appear to have found him in a difficult situation financially and he seems to have been struggling to make ends meet. Certainly, coping with two sets of important financial commitments on the income from a small village pub must have been very demanding, and as a teenager, Valerie remembers the family often being hard up.

This is perhaps best illustrated by the circumstances regarding the purchase of her grammar school uniform. Many parents bought these uniforms from Clappens 'Civil & Military Tailors' in Cirencester, but that shop was found to be far too expensive, so Valerie's uniform was bought much more cheaply from Marks & Spencer in Swindon and the 'St Michael' label was cut out so that no one would know where it had been bought.

The Eliot Arms, at that time, also had a reputation locally as an 'unlucky pub' because some misfortune was rumoured to often befall a new landlord or his family. This came true for Dad, because it was here that his long series of illnesses began. This may have started towards the end of 1954 or early in 1955 with the onset of rheumatoid arthritis, and Valerie remembers the appearance of the first signs of the disease. Dad was working at the time in the cellar, hammering a spile into the top of the barrel as it lay on the stillage. His wrist began to hurt during this task and started to swell, so he thought he had sprained it. Mum put a bandage on the wrist, but it didn't get any better and stayed swollen and painful. Eventually, with no improvement in the condition of the wrist, Dad went to see the doctor, who arranged for it to be X-rayed. This revealed the early stages of the arthritic disease.

Rheumatoid arthritis is an inflammation of the joints in the body which results in damage to the joint linings and cartilage, causing the two opposing bones to erode. The exact cause of the inflammation is still unknown, but it is very debilitating and has no known cure. The disease seriously affected the joints in both his hands and feet, so it is easy to see that he and Mum would think that the effect of such a distressing and painful disease could prevent him from working properly as a pub landlord, although in the end this essentially turned out not to be the case. The illness must also have caused Dad great psychological anguish, because he had always been so physically fit in the past, and the arthritis now reduced him to considerable physical dependency on others. The beginning of this illness, coupled with the financial difficulties which Dad and Mum were facing, may also have caused them to consider a move away from the pub.

Accordingly, and probably at some point during the spring of 1955, Dad and Mum eventually decided to leave the Eliot. Their arrival at this decision is indicated by a 19th July letter from Dad to Martin Lindsay MP, his former Commanding Officer in the Parachute Regiment, presumably seeking a reference. Lindsay replied promptly, and with great warmth, on the 20th July, writing 'I am so pleased to have heard from you again and am delighted to oblige with the enclosed testimonial.' Lindsay also recorded his regret at not knowing that Dad was at the Eliot Arms when he came to speak nearby during the recent General Election.

The letter went on to invite Dad to visit him at the House of Commons 'for a cup of tea or a glass of beer', and closed with a request to 'please let me know in due course where you go to'. Referring to their wartime service together, the testimonial described Dad as 'a first class man, extremely loyal and dependable'. It concluded by saying 'I can with complete confidence recommend him for any such position of trust and wish him well in his future employment'.

In fact it is quite possible that the arthritis and its subsequent treatment may have made a move away to a new job very difficult or indeed impracticable, because Dad and Mum then decided to stay put and make a go of the pub. And this they certainly did.

Whatever the personal problems besetting them, life at the pub had to go on; and during the autumn of 1955 the Eliot played its part in exhibiting the Bledisloe Cup, won by the village earlier in the year. This was a 'best-kept village' competition introduced in 1937 by Lord Bledisloe of Lydney, and South Cerney had won the section for large villages. At its meeting in September, the Parish Council, under the Chairmanship of Charles Mate, had agreed with a proposal that 'all shopkeepers and publicans should have an opportunity of showing the Bledisloe Cup' to their customers. This proposal of course meant that just about everyone in the village would be given the opportunity to see the Cup.

Coping with the initial onset of his illness may also have turned Dad's attention away from the wider activities which he had pursued on arrival in the village. Certainly by the end of 1955 there is no report in the newspaper of a further lighting of the cedar tree, accompanied by Christmas Eve Carols. Perhaps he was not well enough at the time to help organise these events as he had done in the past. Moreover there had been a change of vicar earlier that year; the Reverend Waddington-Jones had left and been replaced by the Reverend Bernard Houghton, so that may equally have had a bearing on the subject of carols around the tree.

Dad also became seriously afflicted by tuberculosis (TB), the disease of the lungs which had taken both of his parents. This ailment and his arthritis both resulted in long periods away from home in various hospitals, particularly the Royal National Hospital for Rheumatic Diseases in the centre of Bath, as well as Standish Chest Hospital at Stonehouse near Stroud. Standish Hospital had originally been built as Standish House around 1830 and at one time had been the family home of Beatrix Potter's father Richard. The property was considered ideally suited for combating TB because of its situation on a hillside exposed to the prevailing winds, and the regular exposure of patients to fresh air, together with plenty of rest, formed part of their treatment. It was therefore converted for use as a chest hospital and sanatorium in 1922 and became a general hospital in 1948, although still retaining the facilities to treat chest conditions. Standish Hospital eventually closed in 2004. The Rheumatic Diseases Hospital was opened in 1742 as the Bath General Infirmary, and remains open to this day.

During Dad's absences in hospital, the responsibility fell on Mum to keep the pub running as well as looking after Valerie and me. Fortunately she was a very proficient businesswoman, having successfully managed a variety of businesses in Bulford from the time she opened her first tea rooms on the camp at the age of 17. She had started that particular enterprise with a loan from her father, which she had repaid within her first year of business, so she was certainly sufficiently experienced to manage the pub while Dad was away.

Visiting him in hospital however was an entirely different matter. The hospitals at both Standish and Bath were difficult to get to; Standish was about 20 miles away, while Bath was about 40 miles, and Mum couldn't drive. It is also important to be aware that roads then had not been improved to current standards and neither were cars as reliable as they later became. Car journeys in the 1950s and early 1960s could therefore be much more of an expedition than they are now. There was also the problem of making arrangements for someone to look after the pub while she was out. This meant that Sundays were easier for visiting, because the pub was closed for longer periods than on weekdays.

It was about this time that Dad suffered from a stomach ulcer which burst at home in the early hours of the morning, when the doctor was called out. This condition was extremely serious, and could easily have resulted from taking the anti-inflammatory drugs which were used to combat his arthritis. Accordingly the doctor sent for the ambulance, which rushed Dad to hospital in Cirencester for treatment. I remember awaking and seeing Mum and the ambulance men carrying Dad past my bedroom door, but the scene frightened me and I just buried myself deep under the bedclothes. Valerie missed this particular incident, being away on holiday at the time. She was staying with Marjorie and

Richard Jones, plus cousins Myfanwy and David in Germany where Richard was now stationed.

Fortunately the ulcer treatment was successful and Dad returned home fairly soon thereafter. His doctor at that time was Dr Matthew Westwood, a gentleman doctor of the old school. No matter what time of the day or night he was called out he was always immaculately dressed. This was exactly the case when he arrived at the Eliot following Mum's urgent call. Seeing him arrive, it would have been very difficult to appreciate that a only short time previously he had been asleep in bed.

Another doctor to treat Dad on a regular basis, and with whom he subsequently became very friendly, was Dr John Wimperis, who shared the same practice as Dr Westwood.

Enormous help around the pub was provided by Viv Cox, who lived with his father Frank and brother Cyril at Avery Cottage in Silver Street. He was a clever and skilled carpenter, being employed by Messrs R A Berkeley, whose workshops and yard were also in Silver Street. In joining the trade he had followed in the footsteps of his father, who had been the firms' Joinery Foreman. Indeed, working for Berkeley's was something of a family affair, because Frank's brother George had been their General Foreman and was considerably praised for his work on the village hall conversion in 1923/1924. Viv helped out both by working in the pub, such as behind the bar, and around the Eliot's large garden. He was a keen gardener and had an allotment near the church as well as looking after the garden at Avery Cottage.

Viv was also a member of various pub teams, such as the skittles and cribbage teams. His regular involvement with the life of the pub made him almost part of the family, and he came away with us on family holidays in 1962 to Woolacombe and in 1965 to Anglesey. Other local helpers were Cecil Huxley and his lorry-driver brother Bill, who both drove Mum on hospital visits. Bill Huxley would also sometimes take Dad and me out with him when he was delivering building materials in his lorry. I remember trips to Swindon, Faringdon, and a particularly memorable journey to Abergavenny in about February or March 1963, when only the size of the wheels and the clearance under the lorry allowed us to travel through the otherwise snowbound Welsh hills. Dad had to be helped, or rather almost manhandled, up into the lorry's cab on these journeys, but he always treated such potentially embarrassing events with cheerful good humour.

Tony Hunter was another who helped behind the bar, while Mrs Vi Binns helped either driving or working behind the bar. Dad and Mum also employed a daily cleaner who, at this time, was Mrs Mabel Curtis. I was very young at that stage and couldn't properly pronounce her surname, so I ended up simply calling her 'Curka'.

Despite his considerable health problems - he often had to wear surgical boots and sometimes could only walk with the aid of crutches or a walking stick - Dad maintained as near as possible a normal lifestyle. For example he was a good driver, and continued to drive whenever he could. He had acquired a grey Vauxhall shortly after moving to South Cerney, followed by a (probably pre-World War II) black Wolseley 14/56 (registration number GL 4137) and then a black Morris Ten (DRX 542) dating from around the late 1940s. Finally, by about 1959/60, he owned a much more modern, and possibly brand new, grey Austin A30 (UDD 344).

Each week he would drive into Cirencester to visit the Bank, Lloyds in Castle Street, or to some other business, perhaps Gillmans in Blackjack Street. If it was during school holidays, or on a Saturday, I would often be taken along, and most enjoyed being driven in the Austin. This was because the switch to control the indicators was on top of the dashboard, and Dad would always let me switch it on as we made a left or right turn. Sometimes he would drive the 16 miles to Swindon to visit the Simonds Depot in Old Town, and again I often went along. The Depot closed in 1972 and became an administrative centre before that too was finally closed. It is now the location of Barclays Bank.

As well as driving for business, Dad would often take us out for pleasure drives on Sunday afternoons. This was really the only free time available away from the pub, because it shut at 2 pm and didn't open again until 7 pm. These Sunday drives often included a visit to a nearby stately home or castle. The many we visited over the years included such properties as Avebury Manor, which I remember as damp and musty; Elmore Court, near Gloucester, where I seem to recall we were shown around by an elderly lady who may have been the owner; and Lydiard House, when it was described as being 'just under 5 miles from Swindon' instead of being in a country park perched right on the edge of town as it now is. I remember seeing it with Mum and Dad on a rainy afternoon when entry cost us one shilling (5p) for adults and sixpence (2½p) for children, and visitors were given a guided tour. Then there was Snowshill Manor, hidden away in the Cotswold Hills, with its huge collection of old toys and other items and where the entry fee was a much more expensive, although more typical, two shillings and sixpence (12½p) for adults and half price for children.

I always think that my interest in history stemmed from these many afternoon trips. I particularly recall a visit to Berkeley Castle which involved a guided tour. Dad's feet were causing him difficulty as we walked around the castle apartments, and at one point he sat down on a large, solid looking black wooden chair. The guide, having described the room, turned to point out an ornately carved medieval chair near the door only to find my Dad sitting on it! Her talk stopped in mid-sentence as she saw him, while he smiled politely at the tour group and raised his hat, which he always wore when out of the house. After the merest pause and acknowledging Dad's presence, the guide continued with her talk.

My childhood recollections of Sunday afternoons nearly always seem to involve one family activity or another, invariably organised by Dad. If not going out to visit historic places, it could be picnics in such locations as Minchinhampton Common near Stroud, or by the River Leach in the pretty Cotswold village of Eastleach. Alternatively we could be visiting one of Mum's relatives in Wiltshire, of whom there were quite a number. My grandmother, Rose, had been born in 1886, the fourth of 12 children, in the village of Great Cheverell on the northern fringe of Salisbury Plain. By about 1900, the family had moved to live in the village of Netheravon, some five miles north of Amesbury in the Avon

Valley, and many of my great aunts and uncles were still living in the general area.

I doubt whether he mentioned it to anyone at the time because much of his earlier life in the Coldstream Guards was something of a closed book, but of course Dad will already have been familiar with Netheravon, having spent two months there in 1929 when he undertook his machine gun course. The course had been held in the numerous buildings erected in the grounds of Netheravon House, the house itself serving as the officers' mess. The building was a large 18th Century property at the southern edge of the village which had been purchased by the Army in 1898. It had firstly been used as a cavalry and then a gunnery school. The Army moved out during the 1990s and the property was later redeveloped for civilian use.

Just as Dad had a close relationship with my grandmother Rose, so I think he also got on equally well with her brothers and sisters. Amongst them was my Great Aunt Lillian Hayward, who lived with her brother Harry in a lovely old house known as Veranda Villa on Netheravon High Street. Harry was a widower, while Lillian had never married; her fiancé, a captain in the Artillery and the man she had called 'the love of my life,' had been killed in the First World War. I always remember Veranda Villa as filled with the aroma of fruit cake, because that's what she baked when we went there for Sunday tea. I also remember that one of the few sounds in an otherwise almost silent house was the rhythmic ticking of the old grandfather clock in the hall.

We also made regular trips to visit Rose in Amesbury, travelling through Tidworth and Bulford to join the old

Amesbury to London road just east of the town. On every trip, as we turned towards Amesbury, Dad would ask me if I could see my grandmother's house at the edge of the town, saying 'There it is, there it is, among the trees. Can you see it?' and each time I would flatten my face against the car window desperately trying to see the house, but failing to do so each time. I now suspect that it was never possible to see the house and this was just a ruse on Dad's part to keep me occupied as we neared the end of a long car journey.

There was also Frank and Peggy Etwell, who now lived in Tidworth on the Wiltshire/Hampshire border, having moved there from Bulford Camp. They now lived in a (subsequently demolished) pretty 'chocolate box' whitewashed brick and thatch cottage close to the junction with the Ludgershall Road and opposite the Ram Inn. They had remained friends of Mum and Dad and had become an unofficial uncle and auntie to Valerie and me. In all these outings Dad was the driver and, over the years, he must have driven a considerable distance despite his arthritis

Saturday 2nd June 1956 saw a fete being held to raise funds for the church. Starting, at 3 pm it would have been possible for all the family to have attended because the pub had closed by that time. Certainly Valerie was present because her name is listed among the lucky prizewinners. However her prize of a pink crocheted bedjacket may not have been entirely welcome to a sixteen-year-old because she quickly gave it to her grandmother. Perhaps a copy of the latest record by Bill Haley & The Comets would have been more appreciated?

Opened by BBC radio personality and children's favourite

'Uncle Mac' (Derek McCulloch OBE), the fete was described as being 'very successful', raising approximately £200. One fascinating aspect of the prizegiving was that the first prize (drawn and won by 'Uncle Mac') consisted of five tons of gravel! The newspaper reported 'visions of a return journey home with a trailer laden with gravel disappeared when he was given an equivalent cash prize'. What an absolutely fascinating meeting it must have been when the fete organisers were thinking about giving five tons of gravel as the 1st prize (rather than, say, the booby prize) in the raffle. Oh how I wish I'd been a fly on the wall listening to those discussions.

On Tuesday 16th April 1957, while Mum remained in charge of the pub, Dad joined with a very large and, as noted in the local newspaper, 'Representative Congregation' at the funeral of Captain E T Cripps MC, who had died at the age of 83. Notable amongst the many who came to pay their respects was General Sir Miles Dempsey, at that time the Chairman of H & G Simonds, but formerly the Commander of the British 2nd Army during D Day and the subsequent campaign in northern Europe. Captain Cripps had been a director of the Cirencester Brewery, an early owner of the Eliot Arms, and when that company was acquired by Simonds he was appointed chairman of the subsidiary company until about 1948.

After taking over at the Eliot, Dad's interest in history led him to make enquiries about the pub's background, and it is probable that Captain Cripps provided him with the handwritten note, now in the family records, explaining the meaning of the Eliot family motto.

CHAPTER SEVEN

SOUTH CERNEY LIFE

When you swear, swear by your country,
When you steal, steal away from bad company,
When you drink, drink at The Eliot Arms.
- George Edward Gaunt - advertising slogan

1957 proved to be a year of change because I started my schooling while Valerie finished hers. The South Cerney Church of England School Admissions Register shows that I started on the 1st May, with my home address recorded simply as 'The Eliot S. Cerney'. The school, which dated from 1820, was in School Lane, just a short walk from The Eliot Arms, and consisted of four classrooms, while a further class was taught in the village hall about fifty yards further down the lane. The school moved to the other end of the village in 1970 and, by 2010, I saw that the old building had been converted to form two houses.

Only a few months after my school start, Valerie left Cirencester Grammar School and began working at J H Webber's Hairdressing Salon in Cirencester Market Place. She was only paid one guinea (£1.05p) per week, out of which she paid three shillings (15p) rent and saved three shillings, so daily travel by bus proved too expensive, and she cycled there and back each day. This was eased by the fact that a group of friends all cycled into town together.

Friday 15th March 1958 saw Dad and Mum have an evening off from running the pub when they took me along with them to see Valerie in a performance of Kenneth Horne's *And This Was Odd* by the South Cerney Players. The village hall was filled, and the local paper reported that the audience watched a 'highly polished production' comprising '2 Hours of light-hearted entertainment.' It was Valerie's first performance for the Players, and her diction was described by the local paper as 'outstanding.'

The success of this production was repeated in February the following year with another Kenneth Horne play, *Love in the Mist*, which drew equally appreciative reviews and in which Valerie's performance was described as 'very fluent and natural'. However a warning note was sounded by the show's producer, Mrs Peggy Fenton, who warned that the future of the company was in jeopardy unless more acting members were forthcoming. Indeed, by July 1960 when Valerie was elected Secretary to the Players, that year's autumn production was eventually cancelled due to the accurately-prophesied actor shortage.

Later that year Grandmother Rose had to leave her rented home in Amesbury, where she had lived since it had been built in 1938 by the landlord, Mr E Gerdes. He now wanted to sell the house, but Grandmother was in no position to buy, so Mum and Dad offered her a home with us at the Eliot, where the spare first-floor bedroom at the front of the pub was made into a bed/sitting room for her. Grandmother continued to live happily with us until 1966, when she was admitted to the old Watermoor Hospital in Cirencester after suffering a series of strokes. Mum visited her every week with Marjorie and Richard, but she sadly never recovered and passed away in July 1972.

October 1958 saw considerable work being undertaken near the Eliot as the double bridge over the River Churn and over the adjacent Mill Race leading to the Lower Mill in Bow Wow was rebuilt. South Cerney is on the dividing line between the limestone of the Cotswold Hills to the north and the flat, gravel-bearing land to the south and companies such as E H Bradley and Hills of Swindon were busy extracting the gravel. This was used in the construction industry, especially for motorway building. The only route in and out of the village for the gravel lorries was along Clark's Hay and Silver Street towards Cirencester, but the narrow bridge linking the two roads was becoming a traffic hazard and a danger to pedestrians. It had been constructed in 1823 and was simply not wide enough to cope with the increasing traffic.

The *Wilts & Gloucestershire Standard* reported that the work had almost doubled the width of the road, and that footpaths for the safety of pedestrians were also added. The widening of the bridge resulted in a realignment of both the approach roads, and this reduced the size of the Eliot's car park along its Clark's Hay road frontage by a few feet. It also seems likely that the gravel surface of the car park and rear yard was replaced by tarmac at the same time. This act will certainly have improved the area around the pub, because the original gravel surface created lots of dust in the hot weather which then turned to yellow, gritty mud in the rain.

The improvements to the bridge were more than justified by subsequent events when, by May 1960, the newspaper reported that some 4,000 tons of gravel were being transported out of the village daily for use in the building of the Ross Spur Motorway. Indeed, it has been said that a large part of the country's motorway network is built on South Cerney gravel. At one point the Parish Council apparently received a complaint that lorries had been noted leaving the village at approximately three-minute intervals, all of them going past the front of the Eliot.

This surge in traffic must have been anticipated by the authorities, because the South Cerney School Log Book recorded that, on the 13th April, the village policeman, Police Constable Spencer, visited the school and talked to children in all classes on road safety. He warned the pupils that the number of lorries passing through the village would increase during the holidays. This case is, I think, a good illustration of the fact that, in the mid-20th Century South Cerney was a very busy, almost industrial, village.

In 1959 an event occurred which, perhaps as much as anything else, symbolised Dad's severance from his previous family life; I was sent to Sunday School. This was not in itself particularly out of the ordinary for the time, and it was of course entirely in line with Mum and Dad's support for the local church. But it represented a complete turnaround from Dad's experiences, both as a child when he had attended the

Methodist Sunday School in Bramley and later with his first family when he made Bernard attend the Methodist Sunday School in Windsor. Indeed Dad had been so committed to the Methodist faith that he had it listed as his religion on all of his Army documents and had once severely punished Bernard for simply being seen to enter an Anglican church. Yet here I was now being sent to the Anglican Parish Sunday School, notwithstanding the fact that the village also had a Methodist Chapel - and probably a Methodist Sunday School as well.

August that year saw Valerie become engaged to Colin Plain at a party for about 30 guests held in the Hut. Colin had been born in the village at a small cottage located at the far end of School Lane, and he had attended the village school before going on to the grammar school in Cirencester. He next went on to complete his National Service at Le Marchant Barracks near Devizes, where Dad had previously been the Barrack Officer, before being employed as a sales representative for the Co-operative Wholesale Society in Cirencester.

Colin lived at home with his Dad, Jock, his Mum, Mollie, brother Andrew and sister Margaret at Highnam Cottage. This property was at the beginning of School Lane and situated just over the River Churn Bridge from The Eliot. Jock, a Scotsman whose real name was John, was a chargehand linesman working for the Southern Electricity Board, while Mollie had worked as a cook at Chapter Manor. This was one of South Cerney's three manor houses and the home of Anthony Royle, the Conservative MP for Richmond. Mollie later worked as a domestic for Peggy Fenton, the daughter of Captain Cripps, at Atkyns Manor.

The provision of pub food during Dad's tenure at the Eliot probably started in conjunction with the adjoining butcher's shop of Charles Mate. Adverts for the Eliot Arms in the *Wilts & Gloucestershire Standard* during December 1959 referred to 'Mate's Home-made Pork Sausages served hot at the bar' and almost represented a reversion to the early days of the Eliot Arms, when the pub and the butcher's shop had all been in one occupation. These 1959 adverts, and others for the pub, were almost certainly drafted by Dad, because they were all in the same general format which effectively became his signature. The adverts were invariably based around a question and answer, with the answer itself including an invitation to visit the Eliot Arms. Certainly Dad was well aware of the importance of advertising, and this is illustrated by an Eliot Arms business card which I have bearing advice and poetry, which describes as 'foolishness' any attempt to 'run a business for a time and not advertise'.

Growing up in South Cerney in the late 1950s and early 1960s provided so many places for children to play - away over the fields, up on the village's one hill, along the banks of the River Churn or the overgrown canal, or around the disused and dilapidated Upper Mill in School Lane owned by Charles Mate. But, wherever I went, Dad's background as a Regimental Sergeant Major always meant that I could be summoned home when required. He used to stand in the yard at the back of the Eliot calling my name in a voice that could be heard nearly everywhere, final proof positive, if ever it was needed, that his voice had indeed become magnificently robust. And if I didn't hear, then it was certain that someone else would, and I'd soon get the message 'Alan, your Dad's calling for you' so I rarely had an excuse for not being home when required.

Sporting success came to South Cerney in the 1959/60 football season when the village team won both the local league and the Cirencester Senior Charities Cup. Captained by centre-forward Colin Plain, who was reported in the local paper to have scored a 'fine goal'. South Cerney beat Chedworth 3-1 in the final. This was played on Easter Monday 1960 at the Cirencester Town ground and watched by a crowd of some 400 spectators. The last team to have achieved this league and cup 'double' had also been South Cerney, back in 1935 when Colin's dad and Uncle Charlie had both been in the team. South Cerney went on to retain the Charities Cup in 1961, with Colin once more among the goal scorers.

1960 was also the year that witnessed the end of H & G Simonds. The company had originally been founded in Reading by William Blackall Simonds in 1785, the current name of the company being adopted in 1885 and taken from the names of William's sons. Simonds pioneered the production of pale ale in the 1830s, including India Pale Ale, which the Company exported to the British Army in India. By 1938 they were producing just over one per cent of all the beer brewed in England and Wales, but in 1960 Simonds merged with London-based Courage and Barclay. This company had itself been formed from two separate companies in 1955 when Courage & Co Ltd had merged with Barclay Perkins & Co.

The new enlarged, company was known as 'Courage, Barclay & Simonds'; and a visible sign of the changed ownership was the disappearance of the Simonds' hop leaf emblem and its replacement by the cockerel emblem of Courage and Barclay. This particular emblem, for a short time, replaced the Eliot Arms sign on the front of the pub, but the idea wasn't really a success and the original sign was eventually returned. The combined name of Courage, Barclay & Simonds lasted until October 1970, when it simply became 'Courage'.

I think it entirely likely that Dad will already have been familiar with both the Courage name and the company's beer, not only through the licensed trade but though the situation of their Anchor Brewhouse at Horsleydown in London. This was on the south bank of the River Thames near Tower Bridge, and almost directly opposite the Tower of London, where Dad had been stationed with the Coldstream Guards during the 1920s and 1930s. The brewhouse building with its giant 'Courage and Co Ltd' sign would have been clearly visible from the Tower. The pungent smells from the brewing process could well have also wafted over from the other side of the river and, of course, he may have sampled some of their beer from the pubs in the area.

That same year saw Marjorie and Richard Jones, with our cousins Myfanwy and David, move to live in Swindon about 15 miles from South Cerney. Richard had just left the Army, and while he was in London undergoing his demob process, the family had first stayed with his brother at Brynhyfryd near Cardiff. When Richard returned from London, the whole family stayed briefly at the Eliot until their new house in Swindon's Queens Drive was ready. Marjorie was a qualified teacher and took up a teaching post in the town, while Richard worked in the education department offices of Swindon Corporation.

They became regular visitors and helpers at the pub, and Valerie said they were 'ever so good'. Richard loved helping to serve behind the bar and working as a cellarman, looking after the beer barrels in the cellar while Marjorie helped with clearing the glasses and the washing up. As well as this, Richard was a member of the pub's 1963/64 championship-winning cribbage team. He also owned a new and, I thought, rather stylish, cream-coloured Vauxhall Victor which he used to drive Mum on hospital visits to see Dad.

On Monday 3rd October 1960 Dad joined the Earl Bathurst Lodge of Freemasons in Cirencester. The lodge had been formed in 1946 and met at the Masonic Hall in The Avenue, Cirencester. His nomination for membership had first been proposed at the previous meeting on 2nd May by Mr N C Richards, who had previously held the licence at the Eliot. The nomination was seconded by Mr B B Gillman, who ran a family ironmongery business in Cirencester. The members present at the meeting in October were balloted on the proposal, and the minutes record 'The ballot being declared favourable, Bro Gaunt was admitted to the Lodge & welcomed as a member by the W. M.' (Worshipful Master).

The minutes also show that Dad came to the Earl Bathurst Lodge from the Border Lodge in Ludgershall. He had joined that Lodge in 1952 when he moved to Bulford and was, in fact, still registered there as a member. Whilst there are gaps in the archives of the Border Lodge, there is no record of him attending any meetings in Ludgershall after 1955, although he often sent apologies for absence. He eventually resigned from the Border Lodge in February 1963 quoting 'business and distance' as his reasons, but by that time he was a well-established member of the Lodge in Cirencester.

The Freemasons ethos of 'mutual help' had led them to establish various charitable institutions, including junior and senior boys' boarding schools in Bushey, Hertfordshire and a girls' boarding school in Rickmansworth, also in Hertfordshire. These schools catered for children who had lost one or both parents and whose fathers were, or had been, Freemasons. Dad's masonic membership had a huge impact on my life, because I was eventually to attend the Royal Masonic Senior Boys School between January 1966 and July 1969. It is a measure of the small world in which we live that the foundation stone of the school was laid, in 1903, by the Duke of Connaught, whom we encountered earlier in this story, firstly during the unveiling of the Guards War Memorial in 1926 and then during his 1939 visit to Pirbright Barracks, where Dad was part of the ceremonial guard.

In the early hours of the morning of Sunday 27th December 1960 Dad and Mum were awoken by PC Ron Spencer. Unable to attract anyone's attention by knocking on the door, the constable had been reduced to throwing handfuls of gravel against the first floor windows before he was heard. PC Spencer brought the worrying news that Valerie was in hospital in Tetbury following a car crash although, fortunately, her injuries weren't serious and she was allowed home shortly afterwards. The local newspaper reported that the car had been 'blown off the road near Tetbury'. This report went on to record that the car had been travelling along the Tetbury to Dursley road when it mounted the offside grass verge, struck a wall and overturned. Many years later Colin told me that the wind might well have had less to do with the car turning over than the amount of drink consumed by the driver!

PC Spencer was a great friend of Dad and had been stationed in the village since 1958. However Dad never let that friendship impose on any working relationship that they had. If ever PC Spencer needed to visit the pub on business then their relationship was always most proper, with both respectively addressing each other as 'Mr Gaunt' and 'PC Spencer'. I remember Dad once telling me the importance of this proper behaviour, and that is a principle which I followed in later life. As Chairman of the Governors at our local junior school in Swindon, I became very friendly with the Head Teacher, Paul Kohn, but when on school business, we were always careful to address each other by the title 'Mr', reserving Christian names for off-duty moments just as had been the case with Ron Spencer and Dad.

PC Spencer was subsequently to receive the George Medal for his gallant actions in March 1961 during a shooting incident. Together with another officer, he had been called to a double murder in the nearby village of Down Ampney. When the two policemen arrived they tackled the gunman, and PC Spencer was shot in the chest before the killer was subdued by the other officer, aided by neighbours of the victims.

Situated about midway between South Cerney and Cirencester was South Cerney RAF Station. Opened in August 1937 as part of the pre-war RAF expansion programme, the station had a grass landing field and tarmac perimeter track. It was built as a training establishment, and had achieved the unenviable record of being one of the first RAF stations to be bombed by the German air force in June 1940. The station was occupied in 1954 by the Central Flying School Helicopter Squadron, and many of the crewmen used the Eliot as their 'local'. When the squadron was transferred to RAF Ternhill in Shropshire in August 1961, Dad organised a farewell party at the Eliot, for which Mum baked a special cake with a model of a helicopter on top and a directional arrow pointing the way to their new base.

The Helicopter Squadron was later replaced by the RAF's Primary Flying Squadron, which flew two-seater Chipmunk aeroplanes used for initial pilot training. They were based at South Cerney from 1965 until 1967 before moving to Church Fenton in North Yorkshire. The RAF remained at South Cerney, and the station was used as a dormitory site for Brize Norton and Fairford until it was taken over by the Army as barracks in July 1971. The airfield and its surroundings gained a brief moment of fame in 1988 when it featured as the fictional 'RAF Kingsmere', a location in ITV's World War II RAF Drama 'Piece of Cake', based on the book of the same name by Derek Robinson.

The family's big event took place on a hot and sunny Saturday 2nd September 1961, when Valerie and Colin were married at the South Cerney Parish Church of All Hallows, Valerie and Dad being chauffeured the short distance to the church by Richard Jones in his Vauxhall. The ceremony was followed by a reception for some 120 guests at the village hall in School Lane, while the Hut was brought into use to display the wedding presents laid out on trestle tables around the room. The date for the wedding was particularly poignant, because it was the 50th wedding anniversary of our grandmother, Rose Williams, and a date which Valerie had especially chosen. She and Rose had a particularly close relationship because Rose had spent a lot of time looking after her during her early childhood and again in her pre-teenage years.

After their honeymoon in Torquay, Valerie and Colin came to live at the Eliot while they were saving up to buy a house. Valerie's old bedroom on the first floor became their separate sitting room, while they had one of the guest bedrooms at the rear on the second floor. As they both had jobs in Cirencester, they were able to travel daily to work in Colin's car, which he kept in the yard at the back of the Eliot.

Shortly after the wedding we went on a touring holiday to Yorkshire, travelling in Dad's little Austin A30, and stopped overnight with Flo and Walter Ross at Beeston on the way up. We then motored on north, and I remember that we visited Scarborough Castle. This was on the 13th September, because Dad wrote the date on the back of a souvenir postcard. We stayed overnight at Bridlington and, in the evening, saw a show at the Theatre starring Jimmy Clitheroe as the 'Clitheroe Kid'.

Visits to Leeds and Dad's old haunts in Bramley came next, and I can clearly remember a search for Grandmother Annie Gaunt's grave in the crowded and overgrown graveyard of Bramley Church, but I don't think anything was found. We then went into the church, where Dad spoke to the Vicar and looked through some large old books. These must have been the parish registers, although I don't think he found what he was looking for. I also have a clear memory of the car being parked on a hillside street of terraced houses while we all went to see a white-haired old lady dressed all in black. Sadly I have no recollection at all of who she was. We then went and visited Kirkstall Abbey, which is close by, before journeying on to Ilkley, where we spent the night. I remember Ilkley because my mum, who could be a nervous passenger, became convinced that our little car would not be able to climb a particularly steep hill and that it would roll back down the hill and crash; naturally, of course, it didn't.

After Ilkley, we crossed the Pennines and went to see Lyn and Elsie Grimshaw who lived in Swinton at the edge of Manchester. We arrived, I remember, in the late afternoon during a rainstorm. The following day we all went to Blackpool for the day, where we visited the funfair and I had a ride on a steep slide and steered a boat along a watercourse. In the evening we drove along Blackpool's Golden Mile, looking at the massive displays of coloured lights. After spending the night back at Swinton we then motored back home.

April 1962 saw the introduction of changes to the opening (or licensing) hours of the pub. Unlike the situation nowadays when many pubs are open nearly all day, the position when Dad was a publican was very different and opening and closing times were much more limited. When he took over at the pub, the Monday to Saturday opening times were from 10 am to 2 pm, while those in the evening were seasonal. From the 15th May to the 15th September they were from 6 pm to 10.30, while for the rest of the year they were 6 pm to 10. On

Sundays, the opening times were from 12 noon to 2 pm and from 7 pm to 10.

However most of these arrangements were changed by the implementation of the 1961 Licensing Act. This provided that the Monday to Saturday opening times would last from 10 am to 2.30 pm, while the seasonal changes to the evening hours were removed and the opening times standardised throughout the year at 6 pm to 10.30. The only change on Sunday was that the 12 noon opening time was brought forward to 11 am. An optional weekday closing time of 11 pm was also introduced for particular events such as the hosting of darts or skittles matches. Whether by accident or design, these changes still meant that the pub always remained closed while church services were being held. This often resulted in customers being able to come to the just-opened pub straight from the morning or evening service, and Colin recalled his mother's disapproval of such behaviour!

1962 also saw a notable event in South Cerney's history when the Parish Council agreed 'to do away with the old street gas lamps and replace them with 45 new electric lights.' As well as there being more of them, the new electric lights were also much brighter than the old gas lamps, so they made a big difference for pub customers making their way home around the village on dark nights. Obviously circumstances had changed since April 1957, when a parish meeting attended by sixty villagers had voted to keep the gas lights. A speaker at that time had said: 'To light the village up with 41 lamps like a fun fair is absolutely ridiculous. If you went out after dark in the winter you would not meet more than 6 people in the village streets in as many hours.'

The year closed memorably when heavy snow started falling on Boxing Day, heralding Gloucestershire's worst snow storm for 16 years. Within the week snowdrifts stretching for several miles near South Cerney had closed the main Cirencester to Swindon Road, and, according to the local newspaper, South Cerney was amongst the list of villages 'badly hit by the almost Siberian-like weather'. This terrible weather lasted until March, and saw regular road closures caused by heavy snow and gale force winds. Both Valerie and Colin worked in Cirencester, and often the only route available to the town was across the local airfield.

During the worst of the weather, the newspaper reported that police checkpoints had been set upon the main Cirencester–Swindon road to the north and south of the RAF station and linked by a single lane for traffic which had been cleared through the snow. Groups of cars were then allowed to alternately pass between the two points, the last car in each column carrying a baton. This was handed in at the checkpoint, indicating that the road was clear for the next group of cars to proceed.

The minor road that led from South Cerney to Cirencester was also completely blocked by snowdrifts, so Valerie and Colin had to walk to Cirencester across the airfield.

That winter also saw ice that was so thick that cars could reportedly drive over the village's frozen gravel pit lakes. Fortunately, despite the various road closures, the delivery lorries still managed to get through from Swindon, so the pub didn't run out of beer. Neither was the school greatly affected by the weather. Having closed for the Christmas holidays on the 21st December it had been due to re-open on Monday the 7th January, but that was delayed until Thursday the 10th January. The School Log Book recorded: 'As a result of very severe weather conditions - heavy snowfall and up to 28 degrees F of frost it was impossible to open the school on Monday last'.

The slightly lengthened holiday did give more time for me to play in the snow and I remember one occasion when, although having to wear his surgical boots and with his hands protected by thick mittens, Dad had a snowball fight with Mum and me in the yard of the Eliot. However Dad also kept me busy helping to clear the paths around the pub so it would be safe for the customers

Valerie and Colin lived at the Eliot Arms until April 1963, when they moved to live in Cirencester. Nonetheless they continued to help out very much at the pub, particularly when Dad was unable to walk. If Colin's job took him away from home, Valerie would come and stay for a few days during the week, while both would come over at weekends. During the times of them both helping out, Colin was the barman as well as continuing to drive Kathleen to visit Dad if he was in hospital, while Valerie often found herself behind the bar fulfilling the role of chief washer-up. This continuing close contact both with her family at the Eliot and with Colin's family, who lived close by in School Lane, also helped during Valerie's pregnancy, which culminated in the birth of their first child, Simon, on the 29th November.

The supply of food at the Eliot had obviously moved on from the 1959 provision of hot sausages, because a May 1963 newspaper advertisement now referred to 'chicken and chips', so perhaps Charles Mate had ceased making his sausages. In any event, catering developments continued, and by June 1964 an advert was referring to Dad and Mum's 'speciality' at the Eliot of 'chicken in the basket' This consisted of chicken portions with a serving of chips placed in a wicker basket, the baskets having been made by Dad as part of his therapeutic treatment at the Rheumatic Diseases Hospital in Bath. Although I was never taken to visit him at Standish, I was taken to see him at Bath and I recall seeing him with his partially-made wicker baskets. As well as making these various wickerwork items, he embroidered the badges of the Army Air Corps and the Royal Army Service Corps. These delightful and accomplished works of art have been framed by Shirley and now hang in my study.

No story about Dad's life at the Eliot Arms would be complete without mention of the dogs - firstly Rajah, another golden-haired Labrador similar to Chota on the Isle of Wight, who had a placid and docile temperament, and secondly, Punch, the lively Labrador-cross with golden, slightly wiry hair flecked with black, and a cropped tail. Rajah was the family dog while I was a toddler, and his name continued the practice, started with Chota, of using names derived from Dad's Indian days. Not at all frightening, he was no guard dog and would have been more likely to lick a burglar to death than anything else. His even temper was almost legendary, because Robert Mate and I often used to play cowboys and Indians amongst the pub's outbuildings (which our imaginations turned into a wild west town) and Rajah was used as a horse. He'd let us sit on his back and ride him for a while before shaking us off and wandering away somewhere where we were not allowed - usually the Eliot's public bar, where customers made a fuss of him.

Despite his placid nature, he did once bite me. He had chased a cat into a shed in Charles Mate's garden, and while cat and dog exchanged spits and barks, I grabbed his collar to pull him out, but he turned sharply and bit my hand. Dad had then to take me to the hospital in Cirencester for an anti-tetanus injection, followed by an explanation that it was not good manners for me to kick the doctor, despite him having stuck a big needle in my arm.

The biting incident was untypical of Rajah and is only worth the re-telling because of my subsequent assault on the doctor. A more representative story concerns Rajah's attending the South Cerney school assembly. At the start of the school day, all children had to go to their own class for registration before gathering in the largest classroom of the school for morning assembly - the school didn't have a hall. One morning, having finished saying the Lord's Prayer, and while the Headmaster, Mr Jesse Peyman, was making the usual morning announcements, I became aware of a commotion towards the front of the classroom. I was towards the back of the assembly, so all I could see was that the door connecting the classroom to the front porch was now open, and that Mr Peyman's announcements had halted amidst much giggling from the younger children at the front.

I was then called forward. Having pushed my way through the crowd of my fellow children, I came upon Rajah sitting just inside the classroom door. It had not been properly closed, and he had pushed it open with his nose. Upon seeing me he came over, tail wagging, a very happy dog indeed. Mr Peyman told me to take the dog home, saying 'Please ask your father if he could keep your dog at home from now on.'

When we got back to the Eliot Dad was most amused by the dog's antics, but he took special care to make sure that Rajah was kept safely inside the pub when I went to school in future.

After Rajah died, aged 13 or 14 in about 1962, the next family dog was Punch. He came from Mr Coggan, who had briefly been Headmaster at the secondary school in Cirencester and whom Dad had got to know. Punch was just as friendly as Rajah had been and, with no tail to wag, his entire rear end just quivered when he was excited. If he was greeting people or just being friendly, he also had the habit of picking up any loose object and running around carrying said item in his mouth before sometimes dropping it at one's feet.

On one occasion two separate bed & breakfast guests, a man and a woman, were being seated at the breakfast table by Mum, who started to make the usual introductions. Much to her surprise they both laughingly told her that they had already met, having been introduced by the dog! Apparently Punch had run upstairs and got into the gentleman guest's bedroom, picked up a shoe and then run along with it to the lady's bedroom. The introductions had therefore taken place when the man went to retrieve his shoe.

When Dad had an extended hospital stay, as in the summer of 1963, visits had to be supplemented by letters. Telephones were not nearly so widely used then, and letters were the only other method of maintaining regular contact. I had sent Dad a postcard while I was staying in Swindon with Marjorie and Richard Jones and my cousins Myfanwy and David. Dad had replied with a short letter in which he referred to a letter he had received from Mum. At that point, August 15th, his treatment was obviously progressing well, because he wrote 'I am getting better and should soon be home again - where I would rather be, with Mummy and you'. He went on to ask me to 'tell Auntie Marjorie that my last X-ray was clear, that means my chest is practically better and, as I say, I shall soon be home'.

Unfortunately Dad's return home appears to have been delayed, because he was still in hospital at about the time I was due to start at Cirencester County Secondary Modern School for Boys on the 10th September. Built to accommodate 500 pupils on its Tetbury Road site, the school had cost a total, of £165,000 when opened in 1962, having previously been housed in the adjacent Second World War Nissen huts of a former American military hospital. Dad's next letter sought to reassure and encourage me about the school, writing 'I am sure when you get to know the school and have been there a few weeks you will like it. I also feel sure that you will try hard at your lessons and get good reports'. However I never did get to like the school, and my schoolwork probably left a lot to be desired as well.

The school was about five miles from South Cerney, so I had to travel there each day on the school coach, which belonged to the Alexcars coach company of Cirencester. All the South Cerney pupils were collected from the bus stop by the old cross in the centre of the village. We were then dropped off back there after school was finished. If I should ever miss the coach, as did happen occasionally, I never got the day off from school, because Dad would drive me there in his little Austin.

One morning towards the end of August 1963 there were just four people in the pub: Mum, Rose, Pearl Kent (who had been employed as a cleaner following the departure of Mabel Curtis) and me. It was shortly after the morning opening time, and as we didn't have any customers Mum asked me to 'listen to the bar dear' while she was busy elsewhere in the house. 'Listening to the bar' was often one of my jobs, because I was too young to serve the customers. The bell for service wasn't particularly loud so, when customers came in I would rush off to find Mum so she could come and see to them.

This particular morning Pearl was astonished to find me in the public bar, bending over with my ear placed against the counter. 'What on earth are you doing?' she asked. 'Listening to the bar' I replied. 'Mummy told me to do it!'

She burst out laughing and went off, returning shortly with both Mum and Grandmother to find me still listening at the bar and protesting that I was only doing as instructed. Mum related this event during her next visit to Dad, who then affectionately quoted it in his letter, writing 'How daft can one be, you sloppy date.'

In that same letter, addressed from E2 Block at Standish Hospital, Dad wrote 'Well son I have been away from you now for 9 weeks and in a week or two more I can come home for good'. These long absences were clearly difficult for him, because he went on to write 'I miss you and Mummy very much. Hospitals are alright when one is ill but I feel better now and want to come home to the ones I love'. A map board at the entrance to the now abandoned and derelict hospital complex shows that the purpose-built E1 and E2 Blocks (later apparently re-named Wards E1 and E2 and forming part of the Lung Function Department) was at the northern edge of the site, away from the converted main building.

As illustrated by the earlier references regarding his contributions to village life, Dad remained a keen participant and joined a number of local organisations. For example 1963 saw the founding of the South Cerney Trust, of which he was a keen supporter, although his support was often limited by illness. That same year, or possibly even earlier, he was serving on the committee of the Cirencester and District Licensed Victuallers Association, the local newspaper reporting his re-election to that body in February 1964. Interestingly, the LVA had recently organised a day trip for members to visit the Guinness Brewery at Park Royal in London. This brewery was very close to Connell Crescent in Ealing where Dad had lived with Mum and Valerie in 1948/1949, although I don't know if he went on that particular trip.

Whenever he was able, Dad was an enthusiastic supporter of pub sports. In addition to the darts team from the 1955/56 season onward, the Eliot Arms also had a ladies' darts team, A & B skittles teams, a ladies' skittles team and a cribbage team. The skittles 'B' team won its league title in the 1960/61 season, while the cribbage team enjoyed a memorable first season in the Cirencester Cribbage League during 1962/63. The local newspaper reported 'the best score recorded by any team' that year when in November 1962 the Eliot's team won 12-3 against a team from the Wheatsheaf in Cirencester. The team then went on, in only their second season, to win the league title in 1963/1964. Nine wins in the last ten matches gave them a four-point lead by the season's end. They also came second in the 1963/64 season subsidiary cup. An impressive feat indeed, and one which was recognised at the League's prizegiving at the Social Services Club in Cirencester on the 25th May 1964.

Our 1964 holiday was spent on the Isle of Wight. On the way home we took the car ferry from Yarmouth to Lymington, but instead of returning straight home through Salisbury, Marlborough and Swindon, Dad diverted us across Salisbury Plain to stop at Devizes. Taking this roundabout route meant that we would arrive home after the pub had already opened for the evening, thus saving Dad and Mum from the chore of having to prepare for opening immediately upon their return from holiday.

Having reached Devizes we stopped for afternoon tea in one of the Market Place restaurants before leaving town along the London Road. This route took us past Le Marchant Barracks, where Dad had previously been stationed, and where he was now appalled to see the sentry at the main entrance to the Barracks leaning against the wall! The sentry's distinctly relaxed attitude must have surely offended Dad's Coldstreamers sensibilities, and I can clearly remember him expressing to Mum his outrage at what he had seen. Looking back on the incident, I also get the feeling that Dad may well have come very close indeed to stopping the car, getting out and tearing a strip off the unfortunate and unsuspecting soldier.

In the early days at the Eliot Arms, Mum and Dad had

provided bed & breakfast as well as term-time accommodation for students attending the Royal Agricultural College in Cirencester. However this particular activity became seriously curtailed by Dad's increasing illness, so later accommodation was reduced simply to bed & breakfast.

The earliest price I can recall us charging was 17/6d (17 shillings and 6 pence or 87.5p) per night, which had risen to the princely sum of 1 Guinea (£1.05) by the early 1960s. The visitor's book for 1964/65 records guests from addresses as diverse as Canada, Germany and the USA as well as Cheshire, County Durham, Devon, Lancashire, London and Scotland. This is quite fascinating, because South Cerney wasn't much on the tourist trail in those days, so to attract such diverse custom was really admirable.

Many guests at the Eliot made return visits, while some may have known Dad before he came to the Eliot. Certainly one regular visitor and friend in the early days was a London taxi driver known as 'Pop' Sawyer, although his name is missing from the 1964/65 visitors' book. I think he met Dad and Mum during their time in London, or he may have known Dad earlier. He and his family always arrived in an iconic Austin FX3 open-sided London taxi, which he left parked outside the front of the pub, and which always attracted considerable attention. Another guest, Mr F Richards from Chelmsford, wrote in August 1964 'Delighted to see you again George', while a January 1965 comment in the book by Mr and Mrs Pett of Kingston upon Thames refers to 'A real Yorkshire welcome back after an absence of two years - just like being home again!'

Two entries for June 1965 were for 'Mr & Mrs Morgan (Glug 4673)' and 'Mr & Mrs Smith (Dusty) 4648' who were possibly old comrades of Dad. Other visitors from his time in the Army were Alan and Hilary Miall from Maidenhead. Dad and Mum had become friends with them when Dad was in Gibraltar with the RASC and served in the same unit as Alan, who was a captain, and the friendship formed then had lasted into both men's post-Army careers. Intriguingly, there were also July 1965 entries for visitors from Dad's Yorkshire homeland: Mr and Mrs Sugden of Pudsey and Mr Palmer of Worsbrough Dale. Most disappointingly, I have no idea who they were.

Of course, with four guest bedrooms at the pub, it was possible for visits by paying guests to be supplemented by welcome visits from members of the family who were able to take advantage of the hospitality offered by Dad and Mum. For example, Flo and Walter from Nottingham would come to stay, as would Lyn and Elsie from Manchester, and all of them would enjoy convivial evenings in the bar socialising with the pub's regulars, who were really treated much more as good family friends. Indeed, I think many of the photographs we have which feature gatherings of family and customers in the bar were taken by Lyn on one or other of his visits.

As retirement loomed, and with Dad's health problems not getting any easier (he was now also a diabetic), he and Mum made plans to leave the Eliot, purchasing number 8 Station Road South Cerney in about 1964. The house had previously been occupied by an old lady called Mrs Eliza Cox (no relation to Viv Cox), but had been empty for some time. It cost £2,000, but was in very poor condition, needing extensive repairs and renovation. It was constructed of Cotswold stone in 1787 (the date-stone is on the front of the house) and faced directly on to the pavement, so it could be affected by traffic noise, although Station Road was then very much quieter than it has since become.

The renovation works were quite difficult and expensive, because the house was a listed building. For example, many of the stone roof tiles needed replacing, but the replacements had to match those already in place, so new tiles couldn't be used. The problem in this case was overcome by replacing the defective tiles at the front with good, old, tiles from the rear which, in turn, could then be replaced by modern manufactured tiles. This was acceptable because these particular tiles, being at the rear of the house, were not publicly visible.

Accommodation on the Ground Floor consisted of a small kitchen, two living rooms and a semi-basement store. The larger of the two living rooms had a Victorian gas fire in front of the fireplace, with a built -in cupboard adjacent. When the renovation work started, this cupboard was found to have been formed from part of an original inglenook fireplace which had been walled in. However it eventually proved too expensive to retain this feature, so a false stone front was created around a new fireplace. Upstairs were four bedrooms, a small bathroom and a large open attic.

When finished, the alterations would provide a new kitchen in the semi-basement with dining and sitting rooms on the ground floor and a new bathroom and six bedrooms upstairs. This would allow Mum to provide some overnight bed &

breakfast as well as term-time accommodation for students from the Royal Agricultural College, the income from which would form a useful supplement to Dad's pension. He took a considerable interest in the planning of the alterations, and explained to me what a lovely house it would turn out to be. As it happened, he was absolutely correct and 8 Station Road did indeed become a delightful house to live in, but at that time all I could see was a dirty, dilapidated old house to which I most certainly did not want to move.

Outside there was a large rear vegetable garden with apple trees and a Cotswold stone barn to one side. Against the far end wall of the barn was an old pigsty, and beyond that in the corner of the garden was the original stone-built outside toilet. The barn was adapted to provide a garage for the car and storage for the coal and coke which fuelled the sitting-room fire and the house's hot water boiler, while the apple trees were removed and about half the garden was surfaced with gravel to provide vehicle access to the barn/garage and additional open parking space. Steps at the rear of the garden led down to an additional area of garden land which was very overgrown and was overlooked by the works buildings of Bradley's gravel pits. This particular piece of land was subsequently sold for housing development, just as had happened with the spare land at the Eliot Arms.

Mrs Cox was the widow of Frederick W Cox, a stonemason and master craftsman who had once been the village's churchwarden, and who had died in 1942. He was working on the church in 1912 or 1915 (historical writers don't agree on the exact year) when he found the carved wooden head and foot of a 12th Century crucifix which had been hidden in the north-east wall. Described as 'a great treasure', this find is believed to represent the earliest such pieces of wood carving found in Britain, and are recognised as having outstanding artistic merit. The originals are now in the British Museum, with superb replicas on display in the church. Perhaps Fred Cox could also have cast some light on a curiosity in the wall of the barn which contained the diagonal part of a 17th century gravestone.

1965 marked the holding of the World Gliding Championships at the RAF Station, which ran from the 29th May to the 12th June. It was a prestigious event, with competitors coming from 30 countries and drawing visitors not only to the camp but to the village, which provided a welcome increase in trade at the pub. A highlight of the event was a fly-past by an RAF English Electric Lightning jet fighter, which rattled the Eliot's window frames as it roared low over the RAF Station and the village.

After the gravel deposits at the southern edge of the village had been dug out of the ground, the high water table led to the resulting pits becoming filled with water, which created a growing network of lakes. These began to be used for leisure purposes, and the village's popularity as a water sports centre began to grow. Throughout the summer months on alternate Sundays the roar of hydroplane engines could be heard reverberating around the southern end of the village in particular as the Bristol Hydroplane Racing Club held its contests. The lake used for racing had been described in an earlier local newspaper article as 'virtually one of the best courses in the country'. Racers came from everywhere; for example Fred Padfield came from Richmond in Surrey, while Vernon Treadwell came from Kings Heath in Birmingham. Both became firm friends of Dad and Mum, and were regular visitors to the Eliot during the racing season along with many other hydroplane racers and their wives.

These racers often used to go out together for a dinner during race weekends, and a favourite venue for these events was the Mill Inn at Withington, some 14 miles or so from South Cerney. On a couple of occasions I was fortunate enough to be invited to go along with them, and I distinctly remember standing in the saloon bar before we all left while Dad, having already given me my behaviour instructions, assured the racers that I knew how to conduct myself properly when out with grown-ups. I used to look forward to these invitations, because it was an opportunity for me to partake of alcohol, being allowed a glass of wine with the meal. Despite living in a pub, my parents only ever allowed me to have soft drinks. You can probably imagine my horror therefore, when we all sat down to dinner and I found that my big sister, Valerie, and Colin were sitting at the next table watching my every move! Fortunately, once I'd got over the shock of this coincidence, I was still able to have my glass of wine. Mum and Dad both thought it hugely funny when I got back and told them how I'd effectively been under close observation during the whole evening!

Other weekends were also busy with water skiers, who used the same lake as the racers. Many of the skiers who travelled from afar, such as Neil and Diana Robertson, whose family owned Robertsons' Jams, used the Eliot as their base, as did the hydroplane racers. Things were particularly busy in the summer of 1965 when the Cirencester Water Ski Club hosted the International Water Ski Championships. Dad's contacts with the championship organisers allowed us entry into the competitors' area and got me a ride in one of the rescue launches which patrolled the lake.

Although there had been no long-term lodgers at the Eliot for some time, Dad was approached in 1965 by Jesse Peyman, who asked if he could provide accommodation for a teacher who was due to start at the village school. Her name was Anne Molyneux and she came from the north of England, so she obviously needed somewhere to live, and Mr Peyman recommended the Eliot. Anne stayed with us for a long time, occupying one of the guest rooms on the second floor and becoming virtually part of the family. She kept in touch even after leaving the village and often returned on visits with her husband, Chris Wilkinson.

Our holiday that year was held on the island of Anglesey in North Wales, where we spent much time visiting the castles in the area - Conway, Caernarfon and Beaumaris. The weather was not good, with almost constant rain or wind, but nevertheless it was a happy holiday. Shortly after our return, Dad took us on a day out visiting Blenheim Palace and the nearby grave of Sir Winston Churchill at Woodstock, Churchill having died earlier that year. Robert Mate, a friend of mine and son of Charles Mate, accompanied us on that trip, as we were often taken on outings with each other's parents. In fact this was to be our last day out as a family, although of course we didn't know it at the time.

Sadly, in September, Dad's health worsened and he was confined to his bed at home for some time. Matters did not improve, so it was arranged for him to be sent to hospital. One of the problems with his treatment was that the 'cocktail' of drugs which he had to take for his different ailments could often react against each other. The day he was due to be admitted was awful, because the ambulance was due to collect him in the morning but failed to arrive until the late afternoon. The strain of waiting for the ambulance's arrival affected Dad considerably, and he visibly deteriorated during the day. I watched out of the kitchen window while the ambulance men carried him on a stretcher to the ambulance waiting in the yard at the back of the Eliot. It was the last time I saw him. A few days later, on Tuesday 28th September at Standish Hospital, he died. I bore a grudge against the ambulance service for years afterwards, holding them to blame for Dad's death.

I was 13 years old and can remember the day he died almost as if it were yesterday. It was a typical 'Indian summer' September day; warm with an almost cloudless blue sky. I was in a lesson in Mrs L Simpson's class at the Secondary Modern School when Mr Cogger, the Headmaster, entered the room. The classroom, being the school music room, was on the ground floor away from the main classroom block and accessed through the school assembly hall. Motioning the class, who had all stood up when he entered, to be seated, he spoke quietly to Mrs Simpson, who then asked me to stand up. I did so, worried that I might have done something wrong. I was told that I had to go with the Headmaster.

Walking beside him from the classroom, we passed through

the hall, where the rays of sunshine brightly streamed through the full-length windows. Inexplicably, Mr Cogger then asked if I had a raincoat at school with me. Looking at the beautiful sunshine, I just said 'No sir'. We then reached the screened waiting area in front of the school secretary's office, and I expected to be told to wait there. Instead, Mr Cogger guided me through the secretary's office and onwards into his own office, saying 'Your uncle has come to take you home'. Still very puzzled, I entered the office and found Uncle Richard Jones waiting for me. He sat me in a large armchair, put his arm around my shoulders and told me that my dad had died.

I simply burst into tears, and was still crying as he took me to his car for the journey home. I often thought, in later years, what a truly horrible task that must have been.

Dad's death certificate recorded the cause of death as 'Advanced Pulmonary Tuberculosis and Rheumatoid Arthritis'. His funeral service was held at the Parish Church on 2nd October, and the high esteem in which he was held was reflected in the attendance, which totalled about a hundred family, friends and villagers. Organisations with representatives at the funeral included Bristol Hydroplane Racing Club, Cirencester Hotel & Caterers Association, Cirencester Licensed Victuallers Association, Courage (Central) Ltd, Messrs Bradley's, the Royal British Legion and South Cerney Trust. Apart from family flowers and those sent by countless individuals, floral tributes were received from the Eliot Arms customers and the pub's cribbage and skittles teams, as well as a wide variety of organisations such as the Cirencester & District Cribbage and Skittles leagues, South Cerney Scout

Troop and South Cerney Angling Club. The funeral service was followed by cremation at Cheltenham, with Dad's ashes being interred in Row 9, Plot 15 of South Cerney Churchyard during the following week. The grave was originally marked by a bronze plaque simply inscribed 'G. E. Gaunt. 1903 – 1965'. The plaque was set in the ground on a concrete base, but was unfortunately damaged during grass cutting and, apart from the location being shown on the churchyard map, there is nothing now to identify the site of the grave.

POSTSCRIPT

Mum took over the management of the Eliot Arms and continued to run it profitably until the alterations to 8 Station Road had finally been completed. We eventually moved there in August 1967, and Mum ran the place as a guest house business, just as she had planned with Dad, providing lodgings both for students from the Royal Agricultural College and for others whose business or work brought them to South Cerney. This was another very successful enterprise for Mum, and it lasted until 1978, when she sold the house, remarried and moved to live at Barston Villa, still in the village but further along the road to the west in the High Street.

As for me, on the 14th January 1966, just over three months after Dad died, I was sent away to the Royal Masonic Senior School for Boys. This change in lifestyle came as a huge shock. Overnight I went from all the comforts of home to a traditional boys' boarding school with harsh discipline, hard beds and basins in the washroom, each with two taps - one for cold water and one for very cold water!

After a difficult first term (I ran away four times) I settled in and, indeed, stayed on an extra year to gain my 5 GCE 'O' level passes. I was initially encouraged by my Housemaster to follow in Dad's footsteps and join the Army, but I wasn't a particularly military type of person. However I did represent the House at one match each for hockey and rugby, being awarded marks for effort on both occasions, so I can therefore claim to have followed in Dad's sporting footsteps to that extent at least.

The careers master pointed me towards a career in Local Government or the Civil Service, and in August 1969, just over a month after leaving school, I joined the Valuation Office of the Inland Revenue. The VO valued all types of land and buildings for both central and local government, and I was based in their Swindon office. I worked there for nearly 41 years, during which time I was made an Associate Member of the Society of Surveying Technicians and then later became a Technical Member of the Royal Institute of Chartered Surveyors.

When Council Tax was introduced in 1993, I moved from surveying and valuing business premises to dealing with Council Tax banding appeals. Until I took early retirement in 2010, I represented the Valuation Office at hearings of the Local Valuation Tribunal, dealing with both valuation and legal matters. Being, like Dad, a participant, I joined the Inland Revenue Staff Federation shortly after starting work, and held various elected posts in that organisation for 25 years. The IRSF was once described as the last of the white collar craft unions, and I was eventually elected as Chairman of its Annual Conference Standing Orders Committee. This lasted until the IRSF ceased to exist as an independent body in 1995.

Longevity has also played a part in my personal life and I

have been married to Shirley for 34 fantastic years. We have two children – Stuart, now 29, and Jenny, now 27. They are grandchildren who would, I am sure, have brought Dad much happiness.

CONCLUSION

I was only 13 when Dad died, so I only ever really knew him from a child's perspective and not that of an adult. However the research for this book has revealed to me that Dad was undoubtedly a man of indomitable spirit. After something of an unconventional childhood he embarked upon an Army career requiring the extremes of physical fitness. Although in his later years he was plagued by considerable ill-health, he never let that defeat him or get him down, and he remained amazingly resilient right up until the end.

I don't know what prompted his decision to join the Army – perhaps it was a desire for adventure. Whatever the reason, he certainly took to Army life, and I think the 1925 photograph of him while he was at the Guards Depot clearly shows a contented individual. His initial signing on for three years was then regularly followed by extensions to his service, indicating to me a considerable dedication to his Army career. Yet this dedication came at a price, and his subsequent marriage and family life do appear to have come a distinct second, probably making him at the time a very much better soldier than he was a husband and father.

Of course he changed as he grew older, which is why

Bernard and I seem to remember two different men. A combination of various events contributed to that change. Firstly, during his war-time service as a trainer in élite units, he will have known very many men who were killed or wounded in the fighting from which he was excluded. This was a situation which affected him enormously and which is illustrated by the guilt he felt over the death of Bill Cunningham. Secondly he was changed by meeting Mum, a woman who right from the start showed that she was very much his equal. Thirdly, in his later years he was changed by his painful and debilitating illness. Finally, of course, he simply mellowed with time. He was a youthful 24 when Bernard was born, but by the time I arrived on the scene he was twice that age – an age when he could much more easily have been my grandfather.

I think Dad's relationship with Mum was also different from his relationship with Evelyn, who seems to have been required simply to follow him dutifully around his various Army postings. However, he let Mum persuade him to move from London to the Isle of Wight, and then from the Isle of Wight on to Wiltshire. I recall Bernard's astonishment when he found that Dad had agreed to the move from London simply because Mum didn't like living there. The Dad that Bernard knew would never have allowed himself to be 'bossed' like that by a woman, but there is no doubt that Dad and Mum idolized each other.

His Army reports show him to be a well-liked and respected man, and these views were echoed by his later references. His years as a pub landlord also revealed him to be an esteemed and popular 'mine host', and the attendance and mass of tributes at his funeral were testament to the high regard in which he was held locally. So, when all things are considered, I'm proud to say that he was my father.

BIBLIOGRAPHY

Sources (including those referred to in the text)
and with special thanks to all the people who were so helpful:

- Gaunt family items and, including George's typewritten "History of the 151 (British) Para Bn, 50th Parachute Bde." The original of this history is now held by the Airborne Forces Museum.
- Bernard Gaunt. By letter and in conversation.
- Don Grimshaw. By letter and in conversation.
- Myfanwy Jones. By letter.
- Colin Plain, Valerie Plain. By e-mail and in conversation.
- Andrew Ross. By e mail and in conversation.
- Correspondence (including e-mail): Lt Colonel Terence Otway TD DSO 1/08/95 (ex 9th Parachute Btn); W Hands 6/12/95; F Bradley 9/12/95; Jack Porter 11/12/95; Harry Ridgeway 17/01/96 (ex Glider Pilot Regiment); Colonel John Waddy OBE 2004-2011 (ex 151/156 Parachute Btn) Len Shepherd (ex Parachute Jump Instructor) 24/06/10. Ms. B Skinner. (Airborne Assault - The Museum of the Parachute Regiment & Airborne Forces, Duxford) 2/02/11. Dr Ken Thomas. (Consultant Archivist, Courage Archives) various dates 2011. Michael Meade (Ludgershall). 6/05/11 & 17/05/11. Brian Dean (Bramley History Society) 18/6/11 & 21/6/11. Major R de L Cazenove. (Regimental HQ Coldstream Guards London) 5/07/12 & 26/07/12. David Chilton (Wilts Family History Society) 27/07/12
- Copy of Souvenir Programme for Trooping the Colour. 1928.
- Standing Orders Coldstream Regiment of Foot Guards 1933.
- The 'Hop Leaf Gazette' (H & G Simonds House Magazine) Vol XXII June 1948.
- 'Pegasus' magazine article by JW & BHL,1950.
- 'The Coldstream Guards 1920-1946' by Howard & Sparrow. Published by Oxford University Press, 1951.

BIBLIOGRAPHY

- 'South Cerney. Some records of an ancient Gloucestershire village' by E T Cripps. Published by Nichols & Sons. Circa 1951

- 'The Kings Guards Horse and Foot' by Henry Legge-Bourke. Published by MacDonald & Co, 1952.

- 'The Red Beret' by Hilary St George Saunders. Published by Michael Joseph, 1950.

- 'Official Guide to Cirencester' by RLP Jowitt. Published by Cirencester Urban District Council, 1956.

- The Courage & Barclay Journal Vol 1 No 8 August 1960.

- 'The Wings of Pegasus' by George Chatterton. Published by Macdonald & Co, 1962.

- 'Newnes Popular Encyclopaedia'. Published by George Newnes Ltd 1963.

- 'With a Machine Gun to Cambrai' by George Coppard. Published by Cassell Military Paperbacks 1969.

- 'South Cerney Old and New'. Published by South Cerney Trust, 1971.

- 'A draught of contentment. The story of the John Courage Group' by John Pudney. Published by New English Library, 1971.

- 'Dropzone Normandy' by Napier Crookenden. Published by Ian Allen Ltd, 1976.

- 'Rudolf Hess - The Uninvited Envoy' by James Leasor. Published by Heinemann, 1980.

- 'Who's who of British Members of Parliament' Vol IV 1945-1979. By M. Stenton and S. Lees. Published by Harvester Press, 1981.

- 'The big drop' by John Golley. Published by Jane's Publishing, 1982.

- 'The British Wool Textile Industry 1770-1914' by DT Jenkins & KG Ponting. Published by Heinemann Educational Books, 1982.

- 'The Airborne Soldier' by John Weeks. Published by Blandford Press, 1982.

- 'The Midland & South Western Junction Railway. Vol 1' by David Bartholomew. Published by Wild Swan Publications, 1982.

- 'The story of the RASC and RCT 1945-1982.' Ed by Brig D J Sutton OBE. Published by Leo Cooper. 1983

- 'Hess. The Missing Years 1941-1945' by David Irving. Published by Macmillan, 1987.

- 'Rodley in Times Past' by M Pearson & M Holt. Published by Countryside Publications Ltd,1988.

- 'Ready for Anything' by Julian Thompson. Published by Weidenfeld & Nicholson Ltd, 1989.
- 'Action Stations 6. Military Airfields of the Cotswolds and the Central Midlands' by Michael J F Bowyer. Published by Patrick Stevens Ltd. 1990.
- 'Pudsey in Old Picture Postcards' by Ruth Strong. Published by European Library, 1990.
- 'History of the Glider Pilot Regiment' by Claude Smith. Published by Leo Cooper, 1992.
- 'The Eagle' Magazine.1992 (Magazine of the Glider Pilot Regiment Association).
- 'Witness of a Century. The Life & Times of Prince Arthur Duke of Connaught. 1850-1942.' by Noble Frankland. Published by Shepheard-Walwyn, 1993.
- 'D Day' by Stephen E. Ambrose. Published by Simon & Shuster Ltd, 1994.
- 'The British Brewing Industry 1830-1980' by T R Gourish & R G Wilson. Published by Cambridge University Press, 1994.
- 'The Illustrated History of Leeds' by Steven Burt & Kevin Grady. Published by Breedon Books, 1994.
- The Book of Mess Management. 1994.
- 'Pudsey in Old Photographs' by Pudsey Civic Society. Published by Alan Sutton Publishing, 1995.
- Oxford English Reference Dictionary. Published by Oxford University Press 1996.
- 'Salute to the Steadfast. From Delhi to Arnhem with 151/156 Parachute Battalion' by Harry Bankhead. Published by Ramsey Press, 1999.
- 'Second to none. The Coldstream Guards 1650-2000.' Ed by Julian Paget. Published by Leo Cooper, 2000.'
- 'The Woollen Industry' by Chris Aspin. Published by Shire Publications Ltd, 2000.
- 'Bulford Bygones. 100 Years of Camp & Village Life told in Photographs' by Tony Guilfoyle & Len Campbell. Privately Published circa 2000.
- 'All Hallows, South Cerney' by Michael Oakshott. Published by South Cerney Trust, 2002.
- 'The day the Devils dropped in' by Neil Barber. Published by Leo Cooper, 2002.
- 'Devizes and Central Wiltshire' by John Chandler. Published by Hobnob Press, 2003.

BIBLIOGRAPHY

- Ministry of Works 'Guidebook to the Tower of London' (1962) & Historic Royal Palaces Guidebook (2005). Conversation with Yeoman Warders 14/2/2006.

- 'Pub Beer Mugs and Glasses' by Hugh Rock. Published by Shire Books, 2006.

- '156 Parachute Battalion From Delhi to Arnhem' by John O'Reilly. Published by Thoroton Publishing 2009.

- 'The British Soldier of the Second World War' by Peter Doyle. Shire Publications 2009.

- 'Churchill's Spearhead. The development of Britain's Airborne Forces during World War II' by John Greenacre. Published by Pen & Sword, 2010.

- 'Life Below Stairs. True Lives Of Edwardian Servants' by Alison Maloney. Published by Michael O'Mara Books Ltd. 2011.

- '9th Battalion The Parachute Regiment. Normandy 1944. The first 6 days.' by Lt General Sir Napier Crookenden KCB DSO OBE. Undated.

- 'Bramley. The Village That Disappeared' by The Bramley History Society. Undated.

- 'A brief history of the District Grand Lodge of Gibraltar' by W.Bro. K Sheriff. (Undated Internet article).

- 'The Guards and Caterham. The Soldiers Story'. Edited by Ronald Melvin. Published by Guardroom Publications. Undated.

- 'Lydiard Park and Mansion Swindon' published by Swindon Corporation. Undated.

- Wilts & Gloucestershire Standard: Various editions 1953 – 1965.

- Wilts Gazette & Herald 18/11/1971.

- Websites: www.a2a.org.uk www.arnhemarchive.org www.bbc.co.uk www.bob.mount.btinternet.co.uk www.british-history.ac.uk www.bygonz.co.uk www.geocities.org/caterham www.imagesofengland.org www.ornebridgehead.org www.paradata.org.uk www.regiments.org/deploy/uk/guards. www.timesonline.co.uk www.wikpedia.org www.gibraltar.gi www.findmypast.com www.ancestry.co.uk www.visionofbritain.org.uk www.carlscam.com www.gracesguide.co.uk www.calverleyinfo.com www.nhs.co.uk www.canbush.com www.lawteacher.net www.britishonlinearchives.co.uk www.vickersmachinegun.co.uk

- Records from Courage & Co Archives: H&G Simonds Estates History Ledger (Extracts)

BIBLIOGRAPHY

- Records from Gloucestershire Archives: D8078/1/2 (Cirencester - Earl Bathurst Lodge Minutes 1954-1964); GDR/T1/146 (South Cerney Tithe Map); HO36 (Access to Archives Website Summary History of Standish Hospital); P71 MI 11 (South Cerney Burial Register Resource & Graveyard Map); S71/1/4 (South Cerney School Log Book 1934-1965); S71/1/5 (South Cerney School Log Book 1965-1998); S71/2/4 (South Cerney School Admission Register 1954-1967).

- Records from Marstons PLC Wolverhampton: Deeds Packet for the Eliot Arms.

- Records from the National Archives: CAB/65/18/29 (War Cabinet Meeting 15 May 1941); WO88/7 (District Courts Martial Registers. India 1937-1945) WO106 (Cypher telegram from Secretary of State to Government of India dated 17 June 1941); WO166/10503 (6th Airborne Division May-Dec 1943); WO166/10730 (3rd Parachute Brigade War Diary 1943); WO169/5080 (156 Parachute Btn War Diary); WO169/10351 (9th Parachute Btn War Diary Jan-Dec 1943); WO171/1242 (9th Parachute Btn War Diary, Jan-Dec 1944); WO266/33 (Quarterly Historical Reports 33 Coy RASC 1946); WO266/27 (Quarterly Historical Reports HQ RASC Services Gibraltar 1947); WO379/19 (Coldstream Guards 1914-1960). WO 379/77 (Parachute Regiment 1940-1967).

- Records from the National Army Museum & the British Library: The Household Brigade Magazine. Various editions 1925 – 1941.

- Records from Nottinghamshire Archives: Register of Electors for the City of Nottingham, South Division, Castle Ward, Polling District D. 1929.

- Records from South Cerney Parish Council: Minute Book for May 1955.

- Records from the Wiltshire & Swindon History Centre: Various maps of Bulford Camp, Wiltshire.

Printed in Great Britain
by Amazon